T0294819

How to Lead Without Domineering

How to Lead Without Domineering

29 Smart Leadership Rules

Rolf Arnold

English translation of:
Wie man führt, ohne zu dominieren
29 Regeln für ein kluges Leadership

ROWMAN & LITTLEFIELD EDUCATION
A division of
ROWMAN & LITTLEFIELD PUBLISHERS, INC.
Lanham • New York • Toronto • Plymouth, UK

Published by Rowman & Littlefield Education
A division of Rowman & Littlefield Publishers, Inc.
A wholly owned subsidiary of The Rowman & Littlefield Publishing Group, Inc.
4501 Forbes Boulevard, Suite 200, Lanham, Maryland 20706
www.rowman.com

10 Thornbury Road, Plymouth PL6 7PP, United Kingdom

British Library Cataloguing in Publication Information Available

Library of Congress Cataloging-in-Publication Data

Arnold, Rolf, 1952–
 How to lead without domineering : 29 smart leadership rules / Rolf Arnold.
  pages cm
 Includes bibliographical references.
 ISBN 978-1-4758-0972-5 (cloth : alk. paper)—ISBN 978-1-4758-0973-2 (pbk. : alk.
paper)—ISBN 978-1-4758-0974-9 (electronic) 1. Leadership. 2. Management.
I. Title.
HD57.7.A766 2014
658.4'092—dc23

                                                              2014008577

♾ ™ The paper used in this publication meets the minimum requirements of American
National Standard for Information Sciences—Permanence of Paper for Printed Library
Materials, ANSI/NISO Z39.48-1992.

Printed in the United States of America

Table of Contents

Preface

"To lead" (German: "Führen") is an unpopular verb, especially because of its history in the German-speaking world. The aversion there even extends to related terms like leader, leadership, or even to those who are led. In Germany, these words are rarely heard because they evoke unpleasant memories and the images of a ruthless, domineering society with all its cruelty and inhumanity, in which people became passive followers of orders. The words themselves did not cause the memories they evoke, and yet they have become contaminated or even outdated and stale. However, by avoiding "leadership" and restraining our speech, we become speech*less* and this is a problem in a world where leaders do exist. We speak instead of managers, directors, supervisors, team chiefs, etc., without truly referring to the process of leadership, which is always two things: goal setting *and* the exercise of power.

This speechlessness threatens to become thoughtlessness. The case can be made that this collective lack of terminology is also partially responsible when we frequently find ourselves unable to exert a claim to leadership and reach our goals through cooperation with others. What we experience at those moments can be illustrated by paraphrasing Jean Paul Sartre (1960, p. 123), who once said, "Leadership slips beyond my grasp not because I do not practice it, but because others do it as well!" This tells us that leadership is always interactive and dependent not only on the cooperation and participation of others, but also on an ability to self-reflect and compromise. The effectiveness of a leader depends equally on the behavior of the leader and of those being led. No one wants to follow some rallying cry that so often has a military tone, but to little effect.

Leadership problems can often be traced back to faulty interaction among the players, and the different ideas as to roles, responsibilities, and overall direction; leadership invariably fails when there is no consensus on these matters. Leadership also goes awry when the other is not convinced but is expected to carry out the decisions anyway. It is this resistance on the part of others that defeats even the most motivated effort to apply the newest leadership concepts and recommendations (see Happich, 2011; Mahlmann, 2011; Neubarth, 2011).

During a leadership workshop, a young manager related her often fruitless efforts: "Somehow I always end up literally having to woo the people in my department over to my ideas just to get them to do what I ask of them. In meetings, I am sometimes the one who has to explain why a particular action directed by the management, or that I suggest, is really necessary. I find this tedious and really arrogant on their part. After all, it is my neck on the line if we fail to meet expectations. Once I pounded on the table and said that I would not put up with this constant second-guessing anymore—but it weakened my position rather than strengthening it. To be honest, leadership is no fun anymore."

Of course, leadership presupposes certain skills on the part of the leader, but it also requires legitimation. It can be said that legitimation simply by means of appointment is less powerful as time passes. Employees expect an appointed leader to perform the job well—however, they might increasingly come to believe that they themselves could do a better job. The American sociologist Richard Sennett discussed this phenomenon in his speech for the opening of the House of Cultures in Berlin in March 2011. He found that 50 percent of the employees surveyed felt they could do their boss's job better than the bosses themselves (Sennett, 2011, p. 56). Mistrusting the boss's ability is not unusual and debating whether such assessments are correct or simply presumptuous is not constructive here. The real lesson is something else: Leaders today must assume their competence and legitimacy will be questioned. They must be concerned about the credibility of their leadership style. Credible leadership is of the kind that knows what to do—especially, in a difficult decision-making situation.

A "smart leader" knows that it is necessary to establish the legitimacy of each decision as well as the overall claim over and over again. It is essential for the leader to have clear perspectives and binding agreements about leadership decisions, but this alone is no longer a guarantee for successful leadership. It is much more important that the leader is able to identify and build relationships, develop teams, and manage conflict and dissent. In other words, leadership is provided by an individual person and that is why the personality of a supervisor, manager, or director forms the foundation on which others can accept the claim to leadership and respond positively to their actions.

Power plays, control, and threats may have some immediate effect, but this does not encourage the long-term synergies that are the expression of successful leadership. Smart leadership thrives because leaders are able to affect something that can only come from those being lead: namely, trust, confidence, and cooperation. This is what the neurobiologist Gerald Hüther had in mind when he said, "No one is convinced from the outside, at best only temporarily. Conviction comes from within, from one's own internal motives" (Hüther, 2011, p. 46).

Smart leadership is therefore indirect leadership. It promotes contexts, shapes relationships, creates spirit, and rarely relies on the words and instruments of power. Effective leadership also knows that if it has to revert to these old sources of power, it has already failed: it has failed to elicit the necessary response in the majority of employees.

Smart leadership is always concerned with the design of a paradoxical constellation: it cannot manufacture acceptance, openness, and a cooperative spirit, yet it is responsible for ensuring such systemic openings can exist and are put in place.

Smart leadership is (and will remain) a risky proposition because leaders do not operate in a world of "if-then" certainty. This *indeterminacy of leadership* continually tests those who bear final responsibility. Leaders must be able to rise to such challenges in order to deliver what is expected of them by others. This requires knowledge of career and team development as well as project management, but also a good portion of thoughtfulness, self-reflection, and self-awareness.

The following book offers a toolbox of twenty-nine rules for smart and effective leadership. These rules can be used to develop successful approaches to typical leadership challenges. Some rules come from leadership research, but others reflect the author's extensive practical experience as a consultant and supervisor for complex organizations inside and outside of Europe and almost three decades in various leadership roles.

These personal experiences provide the material for the practical examples in this book, but those examples have been altered so as to protect the specific sources. I am extremely thankful to the many people who have shared their leadership experiences and reflected on them with me. The same goes for my colleagues who have supported, influenced, and inspired me over the years in my own leadership role. I have learned a great deal from all of them, and this has allowed me to develop and broaden my own leadership behavior.

The twenty-nine rules that have been formulated in light of this experience are not recipes—they may or may not apply in some cases—but rather describe guidelines that *can* help to make leadership successful and fun again. The number twenty-nine has no further significance and certainly, the rules selected for this toolbox are by no means exhaustive. The readers should feel challenged to continue the list with their own rules, discuss them with others, and develop them further.

Smart leaders know that they do not know, as Socrates (469–399 BC) taught us. They know that what appears certain to us, in reality, is merely our own interpretation—*our* reality. Our actions are guided by our own convictions as we spontaneously assign meaning to what we encounter and often overlook or forget the homemade nature of our interpretation. This self-absorption is particularly significant in its effect when we have to react quickly under pressure, or believe that is the case.

The weight of this pressure to provide an unambiguous course of action is (must be) most strongly felt in situations where the responsibility is ours and because others expect clarity, decisiveness, and resolve from us. This is why leaders often fail to keep in mind that although they are required to act, they still do not know. The following proposition by Christoph Bördlein, the renowned proponent of the art of skeptical thinking (Bördlein, 2002), is rather appropriate: "It would be ideal for a manager to be able to have extensive internal doubt, but to allow none of it to be noticeable from without" (as quoted by Jumpertz, 2011, p. 54).

This book makes a deliberate effort to emphasize the "homemade" nature of the rules it presents so as to avoid the impression that they could ever be universally valid. In addition to rule number twenty-nine, which expresses the fundamentally incomplete nature of a collection of smart leadership rules, the rules are introduced using a narrative presentation technique that may appear superimposed, for example the repeated use of acronyms and mnemonic devices. These constructions only work in the German language,[1] illustrating the work-in-progress character and the limited validity of such constructions.

Finally, the numerous examples and anecdotes collected from my own research and leadership experience should be viewed as my own empirical reality without presuming that anything universally valid can be derived. Smart leadership is aware that reality is contingent and multi-faceted, and that we are only able to approach it through our own experience and reflection. In the process of reflecting, we can allow ourselves to be stimulated or irritated by others, even by other researchers, students of leadership, and advisers. This book is an invitation to scientific reflection, which after all, is just a specific kind of reflection.

Smart leadership is "self-including leadership": It is aware of its own ignorance and knows the material and patterns that sustain this self-certainty.[2] That is why it must be concerned as much with self-reflection and self-development as it is with clarity, transparency, and consistency. Smart leadership is about searching—not finding. Its rules apply to the search (in the context of "search and try"), not to the answers (in the context of "perfect examples of leadership").

Rolf Arnold

Introduction

From Transformative Leadership to Transformative Learning: New Approaches in Leadership Development

Transformative or transformational leadership has recently been identified as the key variable in building "high performance organizations" (Heidbrink and Jennewein, 2011).[3] While that may sound like an exaggeration, it is not merely a new link in a never-ending chain of leadership models. Transformative leadership goes deeper. The concepts of transformational leadership aim at cutting through the Gordian knot to find out how a certain leadership behavior can affect the desired employee behavior.

In the process, it is revealing to focus more precisely on the dimensions used to evaluate leadership strategies: these highlight a specific behavior by the leader and what is "effective" is the productive behavior of the team or the individual. Leaders who act as role models, inspire others, support individual initiative and entrepreneurial actions, develop competences, and communicate fairly will ultimately—according to the theory—have a good chance of winning the loyalty of their employees, as well as influencing their willingness to perform and learn. Such leaders also influence the employee's self-discipline and their willingness to take responsibility as well as the "spirit" of the team.

The first proposition (not entirely new, but differentiated for social engineering) is that the soft factors, namely the attitudes and personal resonance ability, are what bring about systemic results—a hypothesis that is backed by numerous studies in the field of leadership psychology. Studies by Manfred Kets de Vries (2008) or those of Daniel Goleman et al. (2002) indicate that leadership thrives on "inner images" (Hüther, 2006), which validates the idea that external results must be based on internal development. Leaders often use "the outside to disguise the inside" (Arnold, 2009, p. 22)—an act of self-incarceration in one's own primary constructs. Smart leaders can learn to recognize, deconstruct, and transform these constructs in order to focus more on the limits and opportunities of others and less on their own deadlocked patterns.

Leadership development, according to the second proposition, can be seen as working on the "inner pictures," that is, the patterns of interpreting, the patterns of feeling, and emotional reconstellation, in which the inherent tendency appears to be: Leaders do not only tend to create reality as they see it (or as they are used to seeing), but also as they can tolerate it. The meaning of this hypothesis can be found in the Talmud verse that says, "We see the world not as it is, but as we are!"

The effectiveness of transformative leaders does not only rely on empirical evidence and the compelling nature of the concept, but on the extent to which leaders are able to deconstruct their own "inner pictures" of leaders and followers. The practice of transformative leadership requires the implementation of transformative learning concepts, that is, the systematic use of strategies for analytical self-reflection ("self-coaching tools"), the establishment of spaces for reflective learning processes, and the stimulation and protection of a continual transformation of perspectives.

Transformative learning is a set of adult education strategies that enable self-improvement through reflective learning. These tools help a transformative learner to reflect on the past patterns of dealing with responsibility, (others') expectations, and limitations (the leader's own and others') in an effort to break away gradually from the old and familiar. In other words, "Transformative learning occurs when, through critical self-reflection, an individual revises old or develops new assumptions, beliefs, or ways of seeing the world" (Cranton, 1994, p. 4).

A group of researchers from the Massachusetts Institute of Technology centered around Peter Senge have done extensive research into the interventions that encourage new ways of "seeing the world" or lead to fresh thinking. Senge et al. provide the central clue when they observe: "By suspending our normal analytic ways of thinking, we allow ourselves to encounter the system directly. But it's still a problem 'out there,' a situation that is separate from ourselves. I think seeing our seeing is just the beginning" (Senge et al., 2005, p. 40).

Transformational learning is self-inclusive learning (in Varela's sense), that is, a kind of applied knowledge that is not aimed merely at perceiving something, but at critically monitoring how we go about perceiving something. In his "Theory U," C.O. Scharmer refers to the idea that leaders and employees are unable to reach their "deeper source of creativity" (Scharmer, 2009, p. 34) as long as they view the world as they have learned to view it: "We remain locked in the old patterns of downloading (the past)" (ibid).

We unconsciously contribute to keeping our daily management routine the same and ensuring that the future will arrive as it was in the past. Transformative learning reflects on the patterns we follow in our thinking, feeling, and acting, and submits to a three-step process: suspension, redirection, and letting go, as proposed by Scharmer. My third proposition is that this cannot exist in the absence of systemic scientific methods—referring to the "technology deficit in pedagogy" (Luhmann and Schorr, 1979). At the mention of this opinion, the German-speaking pedagogy always slides into its own downloads, while the pragmatic American pedagogy searches for new methods, for "Truth is what works."

The initial systemic adult education programs and leadership pedagogy are developed only in outline form, but follow this pragmatic perspective and at the same time experiment with new methodological arrangements like the "sculpture method." These programs are not only useful for recognizing and deconstructing inner pictures images, but also for defining and testing new interpretation. Their transformative effects can be observed on the outside, in order to trace what leadership theoretician and system researcher Hellmut Willke writes: "When you change things, nothing changes. For every change must be self-change" (Willke, 1987, p. 350).

How a systemic approach can have a transformative effect on us is explained in the following case:

"*Not with me!*"—*Breaking down the problem*
In one seminar, a participant reported that he had only been able to attend the seminar because he had checked himself out of his wellness clinic. Queries revealed that the medical director of the clinic in which he been undergoing a course of treatment for four weeks had forbidden him to interrupt it merely to attend professional training. The justification provided was that doing so would endanger the effects of the wellness treatment, the purpose of which was to concentrate entirely on one's own recovery and relaxation. The participant reported proudly that he had flouted these instructions and embellished his description with formulations such as

- *"Who does he think he is?"*
- *"He's not my dad!"*
- *"I'm not going to let him tell me what to do!"*

In a subsequent constellation exercise, a "problem constellation,"[4] he was asked to mark the positions of "focus" (his own position to the internal event), "goal," "the honorable obstacle," "the unused resource," "the secret benefit," and the "future task" with representatives in the room in a way that was comfortable to him. Surprisingly, a scene emerged that placed the "goal" next to the "honorable obstacle" while the rest of the positions were placed more or less at some distance from the action—a constellation that clearly illustrated his inner orientation was ambivalent, torn between a clear focus on the goal (maxim[5]: "I know where I'm going!") and self-hindrance (maxim: "I won't let you tell me what to do!").

The representatives' comments on how "competitive" they found this starting position allowed for movement in the field that not only suggested that this ambivalence towards nearly all authority was visible and tangible, but also moved solution perspectives into view. The question of the "unused resource" (unused so far, at least), or the "future task," or the question of what was really going on, gradually changed the picture and gave the seminar participant who had set up the constellation the opportunity to think about the specific conflict with the head of the clinic. He was able to recognize the repetition of an inner predisposition in the current situation. He was able to acknowledge and respect the worry and responsibility in the director's attitude and ultimately to take a new position to it.

Such systemic clarifications of the interplay between self and others, especially in conflict or stress situations, are usually only able to be dealt with by recreating old constellations. They constitute a learning search in the sense of transformational learning.[6] This search is already established among the methodical instruments used in organizational consulting, leadership training, and team development, and is known as "organization constellation" (Weber, 2002).[7]

The fundamentals of this approach are to sensitize participants to the perspectives and the interpretations of independent observers, stimulate self-reflection, and transform the role of the advisor from one of actively intervening into a process-supporting function (see von Schlippe and Schweizer, 2003, p. 164f).

With the aid of such image-generating methods, blind spots in our own observations can be discovered and the lament ("Why are they doing this to me?") can be transformed into another—fresher—form of interpretation and design: The central mechanism by which organizations learn and are able to develop proves to be a successful transformation process—not set up for intentional, specific guaranteed results, but instead, for opening up options and interrupting expectations. Transformational leadership (see Bass and Avollo, 1994) thrives on the successful stimulation of transformational learning (see Arnold, 2001) in individuals, teams, and organizations: Transformation is, and this is my fourth proposition, through the interplay of leadership and learning, the main subject matter of effective leadership and can only be illustrated here, not closely defined (see Arnold, 2012).

Let me continue to report on the transformation process mentioned previously—true to the view that "What is not present inside, cannot be seen outside!"—and how an internal change of behavior happened that lead to a new course of action.

In the case of the strong-willed clinic escapee, the processing of the indicated conflict with authority took the following course, during which a discovery exercise guided by hypothesizing[8] was practiced:

The participant was asked to role-play upon his return, when the head of the clinic would call him to account. He selected a suitable representative for the role of the clinic head from among the other participants (who received from the exercise leader the assignment of playing the role not in an authoritarian manner, but nevertheless in a manner commanding respect). The rest of the participants were divided into "reflecting team triads" (see Stehli, 2008), with each member receiving a different observation and hypothesizing assignment. The assignment was as follows:

Watch the dialogue between the clinic head and the clinic runaway and develop hypotheses about:

- *Who or what is the latter "remaining true to" in his manner of thinking, feeling, and acting (Triad A)?*
- *Where and in what form does this dialog show who the clinic runaway truly is (Triad B)?*
- *Who does he claim to be (Triad C)?*
- *What other expectations of his social relationship network is he being truly accountable to with his words and actions (Triad D)?*

After the triads had observed the hostile and escalating dialog between the escapee from the clinic and the clinic director—during which the refugee used phrases such as "You don't intimidate me with your authoritarian manner" or "I will not allow you to control me like this"—the triads were asked to openly discuss the role-play as they would in a team meeting, and to behave as though they were alone in the room—an "eavesdropping setting," as Arist von Schlippe calls this form of "active play with meanings" (von Schlippe, 2012, p. 329).

This eavesdropping on the participant whose escape was the subject of the role-play forced him to witness the hypotheses generated about his behavior. At the end of the meeting, he was asked which of the hypotheses appealed to him and which did not. The process demonstrated that feedback from different perspectives can be extremely well-suited for changing self-awareness and for reshaping self-expression. The thunderstruck response "That's how I come across? Am I really like that?" was quickly followed by a pragmatic shift in the conversation, introduced by the question, "Well, if that's the case, then maybe I should . . . At that point I could . . ." and "What do you all suggest?"

In this methodologically staged leadership development session, the subject was shown how to observe himself and a transformation was able to occur through self-reflective learning.

It opens possibilities "to help people to observe themselves communicating and sensitize them on how they tell their stories—to themselves and to others. The goal is to prepare a framework for self-reference in the sense conveyed by this one-liner by the philosopher Alain: 'To observe oneself is to change.' In ways that are very unusual, but at the same time entirely systematic, constructs are sought out that help these 'observations of the second order' (Luhmann, 1998, p. 34) in becoming useful" (ibid, p. 328).

In this context, systemic adult education is a self-contained movement.[9] It relies on the learner's self-reflection by provoking and supporting it so as to contribute to adult development of not merely adaptive competences, but also reflective ones.

Rule 1

Demonstrate How You Become Certain, but Instill Confidence

Leaders are people who set the direction, make decisions, and take responsibility. At the same time, leaders are constantly being watched, others compare themselves to their leaders, and some others are therefore unable to have a natural relationship with superiors. Many leaders feel isolated and are aware of the open or hidden opportunism of others and think that when someone does encourage contact, it is only to gain a possible advantage for their own advancement. There are others who "stalk" the leader with criticism, hostility, or intrigues—for some similar, strange psychological motivation.

"Since I was promoted to management," a software developer reports, "I'm no longer part of the group. When I join my colleagues in the cafeteria, conversation often dies and I sense that people perceive me differently than before, although I have not changed at all as a person. I am especially sad that my former colleagues have become overly critical of me. Our conversations usually wind up in arguments over some company decision that I have to justify and defend. I always try to explain my own decisions in advance— with decidedly mixed results. Those whose advice I fail to follow become upset, and there have been intrigues and animosity in cases where I was just trying to make everybody happy. Sometimes I long for the time when I was just one of the group."

The leadership position is characterized by conflict—an inherent feature of practicing leadership that surprises many new managers who quite often are unprepared to deal with it. There is broad consensus for a "culture of harmony" (Vasek, 2011), and the majority of leadership handbooks and seminars merely offer suggestions on how to avoid the problem without seriously considering the frequency of conflict as an unavoidable fact that requires a new set of management skills.

Leadership is an inherently conflict-ridden enterprise. Leaders must learn to deal with conflict constructively and abandon attempts to avoid conflict or to maintain harmony.

Leaders are certainly no longer thought of as heroes (Baecker, 1994). Nevertheless, they occupy prominent positions in which they must face not only scrutiny and evaluation, but also criticism and, in many cases, hostility. This situation complicates the development of the mutual trust and cooperation necessary for sustainable leadership. It is this tension between securing the necessary trust and the inherent organizational obstacles to confidence building that determines the leader's actions. This was noted long ago by Niccolò Machiavelli (1469–1527),[10] in his classic work *The Prince* when he wrote:

> A wise prince ought therefore to hold a (. . .) course by choosing wise men and giving only to them the liberty of speaking the truth to him, and then only of those things of which he inquires, and of none others; but he ought to question them upon everything, and listen to their opinions, and afterwards form his own conclusions. With these councilors, he ought to carry himself in such a way that each of them should know that, the more freely he shall speak, the more he shall be preferred; outside of these, he should listen to no one, never return to reconsider the resolved, and be steadfast in his resolutions. He who does otherwise is either overthrown by flatterers, or is so often changed by varying opinions that he falls into contempt. (Machiavelli, 1990, p. 113)

This passage contains sketches for a professional leadership style oriented towards achieving sustainability and acceptance; one that can be systematized in three steps (see table 1.1).

These three steps to successful leadership characterize the behavior of leaders who inspire confidence. Leaders are expected to know what to do and, especially in times of uncertainty, inspire confidence. At the same time, leaders must avoid giving the impression that they already know everything. This is why they must seek advice and listen to the concerns of others while ultimately making and implementing the decisions. This dual requirement is something leaders can only fulfill by means of nuanced behavior, which requires flexibility that can only be achieved through a process of learning and relearning, as well as through experience and a great deal of practice.

Leadership can have a very different meaning in different situations and each of these requirements demands equal consideration. Leaders who instead of clarifying questions and defining the problem appear to know it all and who then enforce the implementation of a decision by force of authority will in the long run be just as ineffective as the leader who causes doubt in the team by constantly changing decisions that have already been made.

Sustainable leadership conforms to the following principle:

Table 1.1

Three steps to successful leadership	How do you apply the following aspects of a leadership style that instills confidence?	Self-analysis of leadership style		
		never	rarely	sometimes
Seek advice	I always seek the advice of certain members of my team			
	I try to get advice from those who are relatively impartial and are not acting in their own interest			
	I ask the questions and ensure that I add no fundamental comments, estimates, or suggestions			
Decide	I make the decisions after seeking advice			
	My decisions are firm and irrevocable ("Everyone knows what I stand for")			
	I am never irresolute (even after making the decision)			
Implement the decision	I make sure the goals that are discussed are the ones that must be implemented			
	I try to involve everyone in the pursuit of the goals			
	I evaluate the success or failure of the implementation			

Everything has its time. Questions, discussion, and participation have their time; decision-making and decisiveness have their time; implementation has its time; and performance monitoring has its time. The leader who exudes confidence too soon is just as much of a failure as someone who leaves the decision open or constantly corrects earlier positions.

Rule 2

Practice Forming the Vision

Leaders are responsible for maintaining the story of their department, class, or office, always reinventing it in new, vivid, and exciting ways. This common vision must always be in the foreground of organizational thinking. The "visualization" approach is commonly found in leadership literature, as well as on the home page of many leadership academies using the words of Antoine de Saint Exupéry (1951): "If you want to build a ship, don't assemble the troops to gather wood, teach them instead to yearn for the vastness of the sea."

This expression is no doubt overused. Many of today's workday routines do not lend themselves to a visualized presentation, at least, not the kind of jobs that greet many people at the start of the day. It is difficult to picture a monotonous task as a necessary element of some greater common mission. However, this is exactly what is necessary: people need to feel that their work has a purpose, no matter how minor the function they perform may be. A true visualization of an all-encompassing common spirit is only achieved if the leader is sincerely interested in the concerns of those performing such functions and makes a visible effort to improve their working environment, making it more alive and human.

Visualization is a necessary dimension for a meaningful leadership style. However, it is not sufficient in and of itself. It must be supported by noticeable efforts on the part of the leadership to secure mid- and long-term improvements to the workplace as well as attractive job perspectives and opportunities.

In one of the seminars, a participant surprised us with an insightful comment:

"I would never achieve anything if I relied on my formal position. I would really have to be crazy to even try it, because I'm no good at it. I haven't had any real experience in giving orders, supervision, and monitoring feedback.

Instead, my department runs really well when we sit down together and review what we are doing. For example, a colleague recently began the day with the question, 'Do you know what our building and home loans are really for? We do it to give children happier lives and ensure that families can have their own homes.'

Of course, what she said was no different from the familiar advertising slogan of a competitor institution, but the way she said it was much more detailed. She didn't just say, 'We're putting a home in your future.' She spoke of children and families. I have to admit that I went about my work that day with a smile on my face—somehow my work was no longer so automatic and routine. That is why, in my opinion, we as leaders have to create a tangible connection to the thing that connects us to others—either through our work or our products."

This participant had unknowingly provided a clear description of the major requirement for visualization in leadership. Visualization always consists of the four steps in Table 2.1.

In his book *The Spirit of Leadership*, Harrison Owen analyzed the power of soft leadership and cooperation and wrote: "It may be true that while leaders have a great many practical responsibilities, the most important of these is to raise the "spirit" (Owen, 2008, p. 56).

This responsibility requires an ability to step back, seek input, shape things, and show the way. Every leader must systematically strive to develop these qualities for themselves.

Table 2.1

The 4 S's of visualization	To what extent do you already apply the 4 S-activities of visualization?	never	rarely	some-times	often
Step back	I regularly take time out to reflect on three or four of the most important strategic components of our work				
	I purposely look for what is going on outside our workplace and know exactly what others expect of us and what we expect of ourselves				
	I practice developing creative images of our purpose and function				
Seek input	I speak regularly and purposefully with employees responsible for a wide variety of tasks				
	I ask about their personal goals and wishes relative to their work				
	I ensure that I am the one saying the least in these conversations				
Shape things	I am visibly concerned with broadening their job perspectives and ensuring job security				
	I motivate and initiate through unexpected actions (presentations, excursions, workshops) for the purpose of anchoring new ideas and processes				
	I listen to new demands and goals and attempt to link them to the expectations and professional requirements of those involved				
Show the way	I try to get a new topic to develop as if it is a common concept from within, even if the expectation is placed on us from the outside				
	I practice telling our story the way the employees would tell it				
	I try to develop new and fitting slogans that provide employees a source of direction and pride				

Note: Grade yourself critically and honestly on the items on this checklist. For those items that lie in a "some-times" or "often" area, try to develop a greater sensibility through "targeted focus" (see Rule 4). Rules 5–17 will also help you with this.

Rule 3

Identify and Reinforce
Talent and Potential

Years ago, the renowned German pedagogue Hartmut von Hentig cautioned that it was necessary to "rethink school" (von Hentig, 1993) on the grounds that previous efforts at educating future generations had been accompanied by risk and side effects and, in many respects, had failed to meet expectations. He later shocked experts, in particular because educational policy makers rejected his advice, by proposing that children be taken out of school for some period and placed on "probation" under a social responsibility (i.e., to be educated through life experience).

A fundamental skepticism of the traditional educational practices has developed in recent years due to new research into talent, which provides a large body of evidence suggesting that talent is something that is learned. The book by Werner Siefer with the encouraging title *The Genius in Me* (Siefer, 2009) relates numerous examples and research findings that are all quite well suited to cause a revision of the familiar ideas about whether talent is inborn or is something that can be promoted and trained. Siefer goes deeper into the results of neurological research as well as international talent research to prove that such arguments are mostly based on mere assertions rather than on reliable data.

Talented people—whether great tennis players or great musicians—are, more than anything else, "masters of practice." Behind every talented person there is a period of intense, often excruciating effort. Siefer's examples range from Boris Becker and Steffi Graf to world chess champions to savants of any type, and all support the theory that "talent is learned."

For example, it was Wolfgang Amadeus Mozart's early passion for practice, encouraged and compelled by his father, and not some exceptional inborn talent that gave him the foundation of his musical originality and greatness. He did not create what can truly be considered his own music until he was twenty-one, after an extended period of practice. Upon closer scrutiny, his early pieces, according to the genius researcher Michael J. Howe, turn out to be finger exercises and imitations of others.

Recent research shows that talent comes into existence and matures not from some innate source, but from practical exercise—an important indication of the importance of the educational structures and workplaces in our society.

This view is reinforced by Daniel Coyle in his book *The Talent Lie* (Coyle, 2009), which focuses in even more detail on how to create the early passion that produces exceptional talent. He cites not only the revolutionary neurophysiological discoveries that concern the "neuronal membrane myelin," but he also traveled to the world's talent pools, often at hidden facilities, and watched the talent at their work. This "treasure hunt" led him to the soccer clubs of Brazil that have given the world a long list of exceptional players, including Pelé, Zico, Socrates, Romário, Juninho, Robinho, Ronaldinho, and Kaká.

His research revealed that it is the active learning, besides some initial motivation and a championship trainer, that allows the talent to develop. Brazilian soccer players have a different way of learning. According to Coyle,

> The people I meet in the talent factories seem to have contradictory behavior patterns. They look for the icy cliffs to climb . . . (and work) intentionally at the limits of their abilities and, of course, fail repeatedly. But it is precisely this failure that enables their progress. (ibid, p. 22)

Coyle sees active learning at work in this approach:

> Active learning is based on a paradox: If we deliberately confront something while allowing ourselves the right to make mistakes and appear foolish, we become smarter. In other words, experience that forces us to slowly feel our way forward, making and correcting mistakes, as though climbing an icy cliff and repeatedly slipping and stumbling, makes us athletic and graceful without us noticing. (ibid, p. 26)

The detailed observation of the actual process of talent development provides new, powerful arguments for a reinvention of the inside of schools, learning, and education as well as for leadership and personnel development. These arguments do not stem from the field of pedagogy, in which the subject's own power has always been highly prized, but in the empirical findings of research in the area of neuroscience, talent, and genius. Coyle's conclusions suggest that learning and practice in conjunction with supportive supervision are much more important than any inborn ability. The perennial argument between nativists (who argue the importance of inborn talent) and environmentalists (who argue the importance of the subject's environment) has been decided in an unexpected fashion: *The talented ones are the ones who practice.*

Werner Siefert urges his readers to "Wake the expert in you!" (Siefer, 2009, p. 211)—a call that encourages us to dare to develop our own talents. Siefert is of the opinion that "Those who do not allow themselves to be misled by the myths of the gifted and talented and the definitions of others, but rather firmly believe in themselves are more likely to achieve their goals" (ibid, p. 249) and that "Hard work will take you further than talent" (ibid, p. 250).

The following observation concerning leadership in our company is fundamental:

> The ability or inability to do something is of no importance initially. What is important is not to let yourself be stopped or discouraged. At first, maybe success takes pure luck. With growing self-confidence and faith in the power of learning and practice—a great deal of practice—amateurs become resourceful amateurs and finally talents, for there is genius in everyone. (ibid, p. 255)

Leaders should no longer invest 87 percent of their time and energy in personnel searches and recruiting, but instead, devote themselves increasingly to the internal development of the talent and potential of their employees. According to recent data from the Cologne Institute for Economic Research:

> *"Successful talent management is primarily a leadership skill. But bosses often don't even have the necessary tools and equipment: Only 38% of companies train their managers in this topic, and only 24% of the companies use target agreements requiring their leaders to manage talent" (Cologne Institute for Economic Research, 2001, p. 8).*

Rule 4

Use Time-outs to Reflect, Focus, Visualize, and Formulate Your Organization's Strategic Guidance

In every leadership concept, clarity of purpose is of fundamental importance. Leadership is presented not as an activity to be "completed," but rather, as one to be lived and deliberately focused. Of course, this clarity requires both visionary power and pragmatic precision. The latter finds expression in the formulation of the main strategic guidance for tasks that require a joint effort for implementation. It is the leader's job to focus, formulate, and firmly communicate this strategic work guidance.

The head of a large Swiss consulting firm described his responsibilities:

I am most helpful to my organization when I take the time to formulate in simple words three or four guidelines that apply to our common effort. It sometimes happens that I return home after a long walk in the woods and draw a simple mind map on a flip chart with four branches that vividly show and clearly describe the fundamentals of our effort.

Think of these branches as simple paths that I clear of the clutter after the monotony of the daily routine. I don't create anything new, but simply articulate the quintessence of the topics, analyses, visions, and decisions that have occupied us at earlier meetings. This "clarifying structure" lets me go to my team and discuss my impressions with them. Frequently, copies of this flipchart can later be seen posted on many office walls and it gradually becomes established as a structural pattern in the minds of the team. These clarifying images are what I am paid for—in addition to all the operative and quality-assurance activities that must also be defined and set in motion.

This statement illustrates the core functions of sustainable, effective, strategic leadership are focusing, visualizing, and formulating strategic guidance.

This guidance matures through reflection, especially when the leader steps back to view the activity from a distance.

In accordance with this functional description, leadership loses much of what is often seen in the attitudes of many actors: the idea of a central "power" over the work of others—one responsible for controlling everything and achieving everything. This traditional idea is increasingly being replaced by the idea of leadership that leaves workers alone, gives them room, and activates and delegates—an idea the sociologist Dirk Baecker calls "post-heroic management." He writes, in answer to the question "Do you need to motivate people?":

> No one can be motivated to be creative, or to diverge from the familiar. . . . Motivated people do not concern themselves with what is expected of them and the stated reasons for doing something. They are concerned only with intentions—and become confused. One of the earliest and most quickly suppressed insights of pedagogy was the discovery that it is paradoxical to want to train someone to be free because all training presupposes some loss of freedom. It is just as paradoxical to want to motivate someone to do something that should be done voluntarily. The intention to motivate spoils the willingness . . .
>
> We need leaders who stop their employees from seeking the wrong tasks, who insure that the reward is suitable, and who remain quiet about all else. Then we would have leaders that work with people and would not have the need to talk about them." (Baecker, 1994, p. 121f)

Post-heroic management is concerned with the conditions necessary for the work guidance and with creating the space for self-determined action on the part of the actors. It is expressed in the nine steps of Table 4.1 to strategic reflection.

When leaders dedicate themselves, step-by-step, to these nine activities, they create strategic clarity, transparency, and commitment "under one conceptual roof." Energy and cooperation are the product if participants bring their commitment, creativity, and innovative energies to the strategy process (focus, visualize, formulate) and let it take shape.

Strategic leadership explains the projects, provides a certain confidence, and concentrates energy. It does not "motivate," but rather, it facilitates the exercise of the motivation of those involved.

The head of a large educational institution described his reflective strategic leadership in a workshop as follows:

At first, it seemed like I was trying to herd cats—the descriptions and stories reaching me from the institution seemed too much at odds with each other. A weekend seminar for all those in leadership positions proceeded chaotically as I had expected. To be sure, everyone agreed to some extent that we should offer an updated program every year—something that had

Table 4.1

		The nine steps of strategic reflection
Focus	1	Take time out to distance yourself from the responsibilities and activities of the organization and look at them from the outside.
	2	Abandon the microscopic view ("of figures, trends, and facts") and practice a macroscopic view.
	3	Identify three to four guidelines for the common effort.
Visualize	4	Capture these guidelines in an overview (mind map).
	5	Seek clear descriptions for these central activities or projects.
	6	Discuss the map with cascading loops of managers and allow a shared vision by all to unfold.
Formulate	7	Define specific goals if possible.
	8	Operationalize these goals and define criteria, base measures, and timelines.
	9	Clarify how and how often progress toward goal achievement will be evaluated.

always functioned well in the past. But somehow there was no vision of the future. That evening, I sketched out the links between the elements we had before and what I thought was happening on the market. I limited myself to the definition of three key strategic projects that would make our work much more future oriented and transition us away from the routine and reactionary. I was surprised at how enthusiastically my colleagues, who had been running around in circles, signed on to the idea. We have organized an annual "future workshop," as we call it, every year since then.

Rule 5

Question the Beliefs that Shape Your Decisions and Actions

Smart leaders are conscious of the fragility of sensory impressions. For this reason, they are concerned with instilling surety and eliminating ambiguity for their employees. At the same time, these beliefs are not to be viewed as sacrosanct as if written in stone for all time. Smart leaders demonstrate tolerance in dealing with misjudgments and are open to learning new things; indeed, they take great care to do so. A large share of their activity is directed at finding out how others—customers, product users, or partner institutions—perceive and evaluate actions, as well as the services and products being provided.

Smart leadership is fundamentally self-critical. Smart leaders know that the images they create and the conclusions they draw are of their own fabrication. Correspondingly, they take the only possible path: They are concerned with external appearances and perceptions and do not hide behind dogma and their own messaging.

Smart leaders follow, more or less consciously, the suggestion of international management researcher Gary Hamel. He observes in his book *The End of Management* that: "According to my research, only a few companies have a systematic process in place that allows them to question accepted strategic assumptions. Few have taken the decisive step to open their process to contrary positions" (Hamel, 2008, p. 88).

A fundamental requirement for leadership emerges: Leaders must not base their efforts on giving their decisions the safest possible foundation, but should also repeatedly ask themselves (or be asked) the question, "Are you prepared to challenge long-cherished assumptions?" (ibid).

Traditional assumptions are usually concealed within routines in the decision-making process and other activities that have "always been done this way." They creep into the things we, being older and in management, are most proud of—because we have devoted our entire lives to these products, methods, or viewpoints and we refuse to let anyone "take that away from us," certainly not younger colleagues who are fresh from training and, as we like to say, still take an "inexperienced" approach. However, this thinking originates from the entrenched idea that "old leads young." This is based on the age-old perception that it is experience that makes people "smart." Only gradually do we come to realize the disadvantage in this way of thinking and that experience can also make us blind.

This realization should make us think about the truth of the following principle: Experience not only helps; it also defines and blinds. For this reason, leaders should use a mechanism that allows them to question their intentions, interpretations, and routines according to the motto: "Where can I be uncertain?"

In one seminar, a participant talked about Nokia, the Finnish rubber boot manufacturer:

> *I don't know exactly how, but I suspect that the questioning of the status quo, that is the manufacturing of rubber boots, was initiated by a maverick. The catalyst was certainly some cheap supplier from the Far East whose prices were ruining the business. I can still vividly recall the reaction of the company leadership, who had been around for years, to the completely "off-topic" proposal to manufacture a different product in the future.*
>
> *Maybe someone even said, "Where does he think he is? He needs to first . . . ," as is so often heard in businesses. The actual breakthrough, as I remember it, wasn't the idea of manufacturing a new product. It came when the leadership allowed that idea to be discussed. That is the real point: something that has been true in the past must not be allowed to dominate the discussion; rather, it is always better to call that into question so that something new and different might develop because it might just be the case that the new secures the future of the entire enterprise.*

Smart leaders can evaluate whether and to what extent they are in a position to deal in a more flexible manner with what appears to them as being familiar, correct, and appropriate.

Smart leadership assumes that leaders have tendencies within themselves and have consciously learned to deal with these tendencies. They know they must make an effort to define the changes in their environment according to a mature perspective. This is the only way to make leadership an active expression of change specialists who actually lead by example in meeting their responsibilities.

Table 5.1

Dimensions	Self-evaluation questions	never	seldom	some-times	often
Fantasy	Do you sometimes seriously imagine that your company or department could do something completely different?				
Letting go	Have you really given up any traditional habits in the last three years?				
Seriousness	How serious are your plans to let go of the old, embrace change, and begin again?				
Xenophilia	Do you always take a friendly, interested, and open approach to things which seem strange, which inspire, or irritate you?				
Identity	Do you know fairly exactly what areas you want to develop to a greater extent in the future?				
Relationships	In the eyes of those closest to you, are you a successful builder and nourisher of relationships?				
Innovation	Do you really invite your environment to change, and do you reward questioning, criticism, and searching?				
Energy	Are you able to continuously renew your energy, thinking, and actions?				
Interest	Do you really make an effort to become acquainted with something new or to consider something familiar in a new way?				
Death	Do you always think, feel, and act with the awareness that someday you will be dead?				

Table 5.1   (Continued)

Dimensions	Self-evaluation questions	never	seldom	some-times	often
Anger	Have you been able to significantly reduce the situations in which you become irritated?				
Transformation	Are you making an effort to grow as a person concerning your life, your relationships, and your identity?				

Note: If you answered in any of the "never" or "seldom" assessment boxes, it may indicate areas where self-reflection, development, and change might be required.

Rule 6

Stimulate Creativity when Performing Tasks and Requirements

In recent years, the importance and formative power of creativity, in the larger sense, has been the subject of increased debate. Theories are no longer about the exceptional talent of great artists or outstanding scientists, but their daily significance—especially in terms of leadership, cooperation, and organization (Csikszentmihalyi, 1999). Increasingly, the establishment of creative ranges, in particular, is seen as a fundamental prerequisite for escaping ruts and developing innovative ideas and concepts. Discussion centers on the emerging "creative worker culture," which is replacing and expanding our knowledge-intensive form of cooperation and, at the same time, ". . . answering the question of how we deal with constant change and the impossibility of planning in our lives. Now, in place of career and a passion to perform, we find the focus is on self-responsibility and individual life patterns" (Keicher, 2011, p. 8).

In a creative culture, the demands of leadership also change fundamentally. The success of a leader is measured by how well he or she is able to challenge employees to reach their own creative potential. Smart leaders must also confront the question of their own creativity. If it is true that creativity can be defined as "the conscious (or unconscious) deliberate continuation of the instability of cognitive processes, a subversion of the need for stability in cognitive and social systems" (Schmidt, 1988, p. 47), then the rigid job descriptions and the levels of supervision are, if anything, a hindrance to the development of creative potential.

Creativity can only emerge when individual initiative is not only desirable, but possible. A key platform for the development of creative potentials, as the following example shows, provides more freedom of action:

A cashier at a supermarket does not need to call the manager for every cancellation because she already has the necessary authority. This has a major influence on the intrinsic motivation to perform and further affects the development of new ideas. Even time pressure at work can play a role in the motivation to tackle problems and develop ideas. Paradoxically, a medium to high level of pressure acts to increase this motivation because it contributes to the feeling of being challenged and stimulated. It is important, however, that pressure does not have the effect of generating a fear of evaluation or a feeling of being monitored. (Ohly, 2011, p. 16f)

What happens is this: Leadership that says, "Listen to me (follow my base measures)" is replaced with one that promotes creativity and invites others to "Come create the vision of a bright future." This invitation challenge, however, must be credibly lived. Creativity can only develop when people know that their true potential is really demanded and will not be dissipated in rigid decision-making structures and die-hard procedures ("We have never done it that way!").

Leaders often have to assume a key role as promoters of the creative potential of their employees. It is the forms of organizational cooperation and the leader's own behavior (employee-friendly) that must be shaped in order to enable a truly trusting and experiment-friendly climate to develop.

One employee related the following:

In the beginning, we were all a bit irritated because the guy management picked for us was completely different from what we had expected. The first thing we noticed was that he hardly made any truly directional decisions and the rumor soon spread that he didn't know what he was there to do. Instead, he talked with the management and all the employees. He was very reserved during those conversations: he listened, showed interest with follow-up questions, and paid an amazing amount of attention to the spatial configuration of the conference room and work areas. I can still remember that one of his first decisions was for a procurement: he replaced all pictures and illustrations on the office walls, which nobody had ever paid any attention to, with colorful and striking paintings.

He also redecorated the main entrance to the building where our department was located by picking out a sculpture himself and having the entryway planted attractively. When he was asked about these efforts, he said, "I cannot think in spaces in which nobody can feel comfortable—that for me, is the foundation of all creativity." Only after several weeks did he begin to really start working with us in a performance-oriented way in workshops.

During those workshops, he stated requirements that came from him, which he explained (for example, the deadline for a result), but otherwise left execution unspecified, and I personally had the feeling that he wanted to avoid an overly rigid planning of our meetings.

Table 6.1

Leadership approaches to fostering creativity—		*often*	*seldom*
Cooperation	I consciously foster the involvement of the team in the decision-making process and avoid "lone decisions"		
Organization	I encourage self-organization and respect hierarchies without overemphasizing their importance		
Employee focus	I approach employees and demonstrate my interest in their concerns and suggestions		
Courage	I basically trust colleagues to find appropriate solutions to problems		
Conflict competence	As a matter of principle, I observe conflict not with a view to assigning blame, but to seek the potential that finds expression there		
Resource orientation	I appreciate and try to capitalize on the talent, potential, and competence of my employees		
Energy consciousness	I try to ensure an anxiety-free, integrating, and inspirational social and physical work environment		
Stimulation	I ensure that art, aesthetics, and satisfying experiences always have a place in the workplace		

Note: If your responses are in the "seldom" boxes, you know the areas your leadership could be improved in terms of promoting creativity. Look for ways to intensify your effort in using these approaches.

Rule 7

Ensure a Systematic External Audit and Specify Criteria or Key Measures to Provide Information to Evaluate Success

Smart leaders do not rely on their perceptions alone; instead, they are more concerned with reassurance. Self-assessments, in particular, must account for the widespread tendency to "fool yourself" and rely on "faith healing." Smart leadership does not just require the definition and specification of common goals. It also demands the use of objective estimates and feedback. A sustainable and effective system of leadership needs an "intentional set of provisions" that regularly and self-critically review the practical performance.

Sustainable leadership is simultaneously success-oriented and success-critical leadership. Leaders must strive to implement early warning systems to alert the organization of unintended consequences, long-term risks, and threatening failures. The goal is the development of a strategy-focused organization (Kaplan and Norton, 2001).

What could bring such objectivity to your own success-oriented actions? What resistance can be expected? How can it be dealt with?

During the supervisory task force activities of a medical device manufacturer, an employee said the following:

> *Mr. Baumgart started his work here by approaching everything with a critical eye. He reviewed our department's goals and started a dialog about what was keeping us from achieving even better and more effective results. We really liked the fact that he was considering the data so soberly, but at the same time, seemed focused not only on the quantitative aspect, but also on the qualitative aspect—the quality of our products.*

31

His efforts clearly focused on identifying some central key performance indica-
tors that he wanted us to work on. However, some people perceived this as "negative
vibes," as they called it, and took offense. "What does he think? That we've been
making a mess of things here? We were successful long before he came along!"
This is what my colleagues were saying. They also often said, "That is what we
have always done. Quality-oriented work isn't something Mr. Baumgart invented."

This resentment caused the department manager to become bogged down in his
intention to identify clear and viable key performance indicators and make them
binding. Key colleagues suddenly became ill on the days of crucial conferences,
work orders were handled formally, and so on. Ultimately, in my opinion, in the end
there was less energy, quality awareness, and receptiveness for new things than
there was when he started.

This and similar results of well-intentioned efforts on the part of new managers are common occurrences in the everyday leadership. They highlight
not only the issue of what key performance indicators are, but also the question of how to develop such indicators and how to get employees to accept
such measures as an orientation point for all. Bear in mind:

> The advantage of a key performance indicator system . . . is that the core processes
> of each area are made transparent. The leaders . . . who orient their processes on
> key figures not only know what areas of activity require what action, but are also
> "defined" in a transparent manner. These definitions are mostly of a quantitative
> kind which, for good reason, is often perceived as unsatisfactory. . . . For this reason,
> the definition of key performance indicators must be complemented by qualitative
> values that can be obtained from the estimations of interns or managers." (Arnold,
> 2009a, p. 61)

What is true for strategic staff development is also, and especially, true for
the leaders of an organization: Leaders must know which ten key performance
indicators, quantitatively detailed as much as possible, will best show performance success in the area for which they are responsible. They must therefore
be very careful when explaining the processes, defining the characteristics of
success, and breaking down the total package into quantifiable aspects.

To select meaningful and sustainable key performance indicators, leaders
and their teams have to complete several essential steps for clarification and
specification. The purpose is to make the targets clear to everyone involved,
while simultaneously putting the focus on the quantitative values on which
success can be measured. First and foremost, key performance indicators can
show the progress of organizational performance according to criteria that
have the acceptance of as many participants as possible and can be used to
substantiate controlling decisions. Key performance indicators also play an
important role in quality assurance systems. In comparison to benchmarking,

they allow a more "objective" evaluation of the system. Rafael Eckstein writes on this subject the following:

> Key performance indicators are essential for the sensible formulation of targets and can help improve effectiveness and efficiency and, by serving as indicators, can make developments more transparent and highlight irregularities. (Eckstein, 2010, p. 27)

To specify these key performance indicators, the following three steps must be taken:

Table 7.1

Step	Description	Example (product development department)
Analysis Which aspects of the input level (e.g., number of requests), process level (e.g., frequency of breakdowns in the production process), or output level (e.g., ratio of fault-free products) should my success indicators focus on?	If the analysis of possible key performance indicator ranges is to lead to sustainable choices, it is important to focus as clearly and specifically as possible on the parameters (conditions) of the organization's success.	*In a key performance indicator workshop, participants decide to focus on the input area "Demand for further education and coaching," the process area "Use of motivational methods and self-education material", and the output area "Participant satisfaction."*
Definition Key performance indicators are quantitative statements. This means that a desired value (the target value) must be defined.	In a second step, evaluate what matters, i.e., the values that have been specified, as much as possible, in consensus with all those involved and which are to be achieved through a common effort.	*These areas are specified by agreement, among other things, on the following: "We would like to achieve an annual 5% increase in enrollments and expect systematic self-education methods to be used in 50% of our values."*
Implementation (controlling) The third step is concerned with establishing a clear strategy for the actions related to the key performance indicators. Indicators are not merely nice-to-have provisions, but operationally relevant quantities.	The third step is a component of the management process: At regular intervals, leaders must evaluate the extent to which targets have been reached in order to be able to introduce timely measures (such as the provision of additional resources) to counteract negative trends.	*After one year, the enrollment statistics and the course evaluations are systemically analyzed to find out whether key performance targets have been reached or implemented.*

Rule 8

Develop an Understanding of the Social Environment

Experienced leaders know that the true perceptions and evaluations as well as the wishes and expectations of their employees are very often difficult to obtain. At least, such things are not lying about in open daylight and smart leaders are well-advised to exercise a degree of constructive distrust (especially concerning good news). Long ago, in the short but famous book *The Art of Worldly Wisdom* by Balthasar Gracians (1601–1658) and translated by Arthur Schopenhauer, the Jesuit priest advised leaders to have reservations about their inquiries.

> Man lives through investigation. What we see is the smallest part; we live on trust and good faith. The truth . . . seldom reaches us pure and unadulterated, least of all when it comes from afar; it always has a sprinkling of the emotions through which it has traveled. Passion colors everything it touches, sometimes favorably, sometimes unfavorably. It always aims for an impression. Therefore, lend an ear to the flatterer with great caution, with even greater to the critic. In this, our entire attention is required if we are to discover the intention of the messenger and to see in advance which foot he puts forward. Wise reflection is the measure of the exaggerated and the false. (Gracians, n.d., p. 61f)

In other words: Leaders find themselves in constant danger of receiving only selective impressions of events, and then making basic estimations or even decisions on the basis of such snapshots of perception.

It is essential for effective leaders to be familiar with the social mechanisms of recognition, evaluation, and strong beliefs. A leader must be able to recognize errors in measurement when forming an opinion. These are hard to avoid and hinder the effort to see "the truth" of what motivates others as well as what they expect and what assessments they may have already made concerning the common effort. These measurement errors can often be traced back to the "distorting factors," listed in the table below:

Table 8.1

Measurement error	Distorting factor	Solution
"I will only see what I want to see and what I can see." (constructivist error)	Your own habits, experiences, and interests	"Where do you allow yourself to be irritated?" Seek and settle irritations (e.g., in a supervisory context)
"I only see what people let me see." (opportunistic error)	The belief that colleagues have correctly filtered out the chaff	"How do you call things into question?" Ask others and search deliberately for uncomfortable truths
"I only see what is revealed to me and others." (censor in the mind error)	The participants' own unintentional filtering of things	"How do you deal with other realities?" Engage in confidential conversations and regularly "check things out."

The words below are an excerpt from a coaching session:

What really bothered me during the last strike was that everyone suddenly banded together. Nobody had warned me in advance—on the contrary. My department head reassured me by saying, "What's going on in the metal industry is one thing, but the loyalty of our employees towards our company is another. There is no way a work stoppage can occur here." I believed him—not least because the employees with whom I spoke personally gave me the impression that everything was okay here and that there were no real problems or dissatisfaction. Then some union approaches the media demanding a 5% increase and boom! it's all over.

In such situations, leaders often have doubts about their own perception and many take it personally, some becoming ill and disappointed. Such reactions reinforce an image of leadership, cooperation, and communication that seems very atavistic, as if declaring, "If you are not with me (and my expectations), you're against me!" Such an unsophisticated view of the social fulcrum of organizations is unprofessional. Professional leadership works on the following principle:

People act in harmony with their interests and expectations as well as with the formative habits of their immediate environment (their families, colleagues, friends, etc.). In cases of doubt, these bonds prove stronger than any promises or agreements. Employees, by acting according to the logic of their social world, are behaving just as leaders do (see Blumenberg, 2010).

After the person being coached had come to grips with the inevitability of "loyalty to one's social world," he observed,

"It was helpful for me to recognize that I am also bound by immovable loyalties. If my friends and colleagues required a clear signal of loyalty, I would know exactly whose side I was on and I would join them. Now that I understand this, I can manage my employees differently. I no longer judge them, but react strictly as a leader on the basis of 'We have a new situation and we need to find a new solution.' In this context, it is now clear to me that smart leadership begins at the point where we stop judging the world by our own standards. By judging others, I marginalize them and so prevent any synergetic cooperation from emerging. This is the lesson I have learned as a leader: I am paid to develop appropriate problem-solving strategies in the face of constantly changing situations and not get stopped by condemning others."

Table 8.2

	– No Assigning Blame – *Nine steps to dealing with the inevitable social resistance*
Self-criticism	(1) What feelings arise in me when faced with disappointment?
	(2) How do these feelings "cloud" my view of others?
	(3) Can I handle the fact that the other person may also be right – in his own right?
Re-evaluate	(4) What would an appreciative description of the other person sound like?
	(5) What "honest effort" can I attribute to my counterpart?
	(6) What impression must my judgment have left on them?
New action	(7) How can I apologize for the image that I have created?
	(8) How can I approach my counterpart in a new way?
	(9) What other confidence-building measures are possible?

Rule 9

Conduct Regular Exploratory Conversations with Employees

Social science research tells us leadership is a communicative function. Smart leaders communicate in a style that presents their intentions, feedback, and follow-up questions, and relate their leadership style to the concerns and reactions of others. For this reason, communication skills are essential. Of course, it is also important for the leader to have:

- The expert knowledge of the subject necessary to evaluate and judge relationships competently
- Substantial supervisory skills, for the successful goal-oriented management of projects
- The credibility to represent the organization convincingly.

The expression of all of these skills requires effective communication skills: Leadership is a communicative process whose effectiveness depends on the communicative abilities and "authentic engagement" of the leader (Neal and Neal, 2011). Leaders are conveners, and "the role of the Convener is to gather and hold the people" (ibid, p. 1).

The communication of leadership not only concentrates on technical details and on maintaining a professional tone. People follow someone who is sincere as a whole person. They do not wish to be spoken to merely as employees, but as a person. This expectation is not met by simply mastering some communication tricks. A sincere exchange with employees requires leaders to have an authentic interest in the person they are addressing. Without such interest, effective communication is extremely difficult. For this reason, a litmus test of effective leadership is: *To what extent am I truly interested in the person with whom I am speaking?*

Leaders will not be effective if they micromanage everything and supervise their employees too closely; instead, they are judged on their ability to combine the motivations of those involved. This ability is what Craig and Patricia Neal describe when using the term "convener"—one who calls together and adjusts (what belongs together). They write:

> Each voice is needed. . . . Hearing all the voices is when we begin to experience the emergence of a wholeness in the gathering. With the coalescence of intent within a safe container and hearing from each person, comes a more whole picture, accounted for by the group. This is the beginning of what we call 'listening one another into being.' Our mutual generosity, through speaking and listening, is needed to generate authentic engagement in the group. Generosity is most likely to occur when we are accepted and valued. (ibid, p. 89f)

Openness towards employees with all their worries, questions, opinions, and ideas is important to ensure that exploratory conversations with employees are meaningful. Without this openness, there is a real risk that leaders will only hear defensive comments and not authentic contributions. They risk losing valuable information and not knowing "what is going on." A smart leader knows that conversation only for its own sake is not very useful, and that impatience and hasty judgment smother the energies needed for authentic relationships.

For this reason, effective leaders practice and improve their performance in the "dimension of authentic employee conversation." The following self-check can help to identify the dimensions that lead so often to impatience and expressions of judgment.

The "never" and "seldom" areas serve to indicate the leadership dimensions that can be improved to make the leader even "smarter." The leader who does not truly master these dimensions can engage in as many exploratory conversations as he or she wants and still remain alone with his or her *impatience* and *judgment*. The categorical imperative of the smart leader is: Become a convener! Always speak in such a style that your employees feel you value them as complete persons and they, in return, will express their true feelings.

Table 9.1

Self-check: Characteristics of exploratory conversation		*never*	*seldom*	*often*	*always*
Approachable	I avoid clichés and address the person directly, using a personal tone and mentioning specifics.				
Unprejudiced	I deliberately abandon any previous impressions, experiences, and judgments (of the person I am speaking to or the subject matter).				
Subject oriented	I never lose sight of the goal and focus my questions and contributions towards this end.				
Congenial	I go into the conversation with an open attitude and avoid such meetings during stressful situations.				
Serious	I strive to be serious and am aware of the subjective meaning the conversation may have for the other person.				
Firm	I press for the exchange of the information needed to reach the pending decisions.				
Exploring	While goal oriented all of the time, I listen carefully and try to determine the perspectives and concerns of the other person.				
Initiative	I take control of the conversation and ensure that we do not lose ourselves in incidentals.				
Caring	I repeatedly ask follow-up questions in order to ensure that the other person has the opportunity to express anything deemed important.				
Constructive	I ensure that at the end of the conversation, the other person has a clear understanding and knows what the next step is.				
Yielding	I am devoted to the conversation and remember that the goal and topic should serve the interests of the other person.				

Rule 10

Practice Employee Counseling Sessions

Many management books identify having an employee focus as the key to effective leadership. Counseling sessions serve to "communicate company goals down to the employee level and to convey the importance of each employee's function. To a certain extent, the task of management and leaders is to give a sense of purpose to the employees" (Lang, 2004, p. 75).

Leaders need to know the various forms and functions of counseling, but should also be capable of implementing them professionally in their daily leadership. The various types of counseling sessions that may be useful to the smart leader are listed and discussed in the following:

Table 10.1

Type	Description	Focus
Appraisal interview	An appraisal is an evaluation of the employee's performance that usually serves to determine his future suitability for new tasks. The criteria used for the appraisal interview may include, for example, volume and quality of work, technical knowledge, leadership and work patterns, ability to work under pressure, and dedication.	The goal is to evaluate performance as objectively as possible based on clear and transparent criteria. It is not a negotiation of goals or the communication of subjective impressions and expectations.

The roles of the leader and the employee can never be clearer than in the *appraisal interview: one evaluates and the other is evaluated.* This difference and the inherent imbalance of power that characterize this interview cannot be concealed or trivialized by jovial behavior on the part of the leader without

reducing the seriousness of the situation. A transparent process, the explana-
tion of criteria, and the reasons for the evaluation, however, do keep the
evaluation objective and reduce unjustified fears.

Table 10.2

Type	Description	Focus
Delegation interview	In this conversation, an employee is assigned a task—a step that can be motivating and burdening at the same time. The goal of the conversation is to find out under what conditions the employee is prepared to assume the responsibility.	At its core, delegation is a sign of respect – the leader signals his confidence in the employee's abilities just in the very fact of delegating his own responsibility. This should be clearly articulated. It is also important that the magnitude of the burden is realistically assessed and the necessary resources are provided.

A delegation interview can also unleash ambivalence. Although the leader
is expressing a certain level of faith in the employee, the conversation usually
involves a goal-setting session. Previous tasks and goals will be expanded,
which means that every delegation interview should include the questions,
"Do you think you can do it?" and "What do you need to complete this
additional task?" The interview will also include a discussion of the tasks
that the employee should relinquish in order to have the time and energy for
the new one.

The other types and reasons for a counseling session each require specific
attention (focus) and varying degrees of control:

Table 10.3   Types of Counseling Sessions

Type	Description	Focus
Technical problem-solving	A fundamental component of this conversation is qualified feedback for the employee, with comments that both acknowledge success and help identify what are the elements the leader values. The goal is a complete description of the problem (for both sides), and the mobilization of the required internal resources.	The technical problem-solving discussion begins with a phase of active listening (Gordon), during which the leader attempts to elicit an accurate description of the problem. Before offering any suggestions, the next step is to solicit and promote possible solutions and then analyze them together with the employee to reach a workable solution.

Table 10.3 (Continued)

Type	Description	Focus
Coaching and counseling	These sessions are primarily aimed at advanced training. Potential and deficits are central starting points. The goal is a comparison of the company's goals and the employee's individual goals. The result should be a realistic definition of the next steps for continuing development.	The coaching and counseling conversation functions like an *appraisal interview* in that it assesses the employee's performance and potential in relation to task requirements, but differs in that it intertwines the employee's own plans, for development.
Conflict resolution	If the leader is not involved in the confrontation, he can act as an impartial mediator. The initial aim is to develop information that removes the situation from the subjective viewpoints of each party to the conflict. The goal is to arrive at a possible alternative course of action.	A conflict resolution session is similar to a technical problem-solving discussion, however, a conflict situation is not technical, but social. Those involved have generally exhausted their own ideas for a solution. The solution cannot simply be worked out by the two parties, but requires resolution by the leader.
Goal-setting	The immediate purpose of this conversation is the implementation of strategic goals and the identification of key performance indicators for the area in question. The goal is a "partnership" agreement setting benchmarks by which employees are to be measured.	Although goal-setting is concerned with a mutual agreement, the leader guides the conversation with clear requirements and expectations that may not be rejected (although they may be modified) without endangering the goals of the entire system.
Annual	This conversation is often used to combine the six other types and occurs at regular intervals (annually). Its function is to provide an individual comparison of the goals and accomplishments over the previous year. It is useful providing feedback (recognition) as well as in identifying areas that need improvement or additional training.	The annual session is an *exploratory conversation* (see Rule 9), in which the leader attempts to discover whether there is need on the part of the employee for a problem-solving, coaching or counseling, conflict resolution, or goal-setting.

(adapted from Gutschelhofer 2004, p. 1223 ff)

Rule 11

Practice the Art of "Eloquent Silence" at Meetings

Smart leaders have to "show their colors." They can't always remain silent on the issues and remain on the sidelines as events unfold. At the same time, they have to listen closely and make decisions that resonate as much as possible within the system for which they are responsible. This infers the need to refrain from making lone decisions, as so often happens in the practice of leadership.

Lone decisions indicate a lack of dialog and reinforce the idea that the opinions of others never count, or the feeling that "I am never asked." Lone decisions create unnecessary resistance, which often would not exist in the same degree had an earlier dialog occurred. Resistance is the sand in the gears of a learning organization. It can cause even the well-intentioned goals and ideas of a leader, which are based on participation, integration, and the delegation of responsibilities, to evaporate into thin air.

Leadership is a balancing act between communicating one's own estimates, intentions, and decisions, and taking other estimates, intentions, and decisions into account. Therefore, smart leaders must master both the art of speech and the art of silence.

Paradoxically, leadership oriented on effective communication requires the art of eloquent silence. This is the term used by Wittgenstein's biographer William W. Barley to characterize the fundamental attitude of the great philosopher in view of the impossibility of verbalizing the "truly effective" (Bartley, 1999, p. 57). In the well-known final sentence of his *Tractatus Logico-Philosophicus*, Wittgenstein expresses this approach with the words "Whereof one cannot speak, thereof one must be silent" (Wittgenstein, 1963, p. 115).

He refers to an internal approach that simultaneously demonstrates tranquility and alertness. Consequently, the leader who remains eloquently silent may have much to say, but has realized that expressing it openly carries risk and unintended side effects that may not aid the leader in effectively intertwining his perspective with the view of things taken by the other.

An employee of a major energy group revealed her experience with leaders:

> *Earlier, I remember, there was barely any discussion: decisions were made at "the top." The way our department leader understood his job, he was primarily responsible for the implementation of those decisions. The details of how certain requirements could be met in specific instances was hardly ever the subject of a meeting.*
>
> *Everyone was certain that "those guys up there have already decided everything." His successor goes about the job very differently. Of course, he still has to deal with the requirements of his superiors, but he always informs us about it with the question: "What consequences does that step have for us?" It has already been the case that he has received tips and inquiries that have given him reason to renegotiate the requirement.*
>
> *So, colleagues in my department feel much more strongly that they are valued and noticed—even in the implementation of requirements. It is this "How?" they contribute to that gives them relevance and gives them the feeling that not all decisions are made without their input. I have observed Mr. K., our department head, in meetings where the question "What consequences does that have for us?" is to be discussed and admired how he really stays quiet in such meetings and listens carefully and takes notes. He also constantly summarizes very briefly what has been said so that everyone's comments are included. I kind of have the feeling that the head of the department is on our side and really tries hard to achieve the long-term security and success of our work.*

Controlled attentiveness produces trust in cases like the one above and guarantees willingness to cooperate and to participate. Such attentive posture is not only the result of specific action, but comes about through specific inaction, which creates the space for the system to articulate itself and "reach a state of clarity."

Leaders have to be able to remain "eloquently silent" because at a certain phase, silence can provide room for the expression of exactly that which a systemic, effective leadership requires: that is, leadership "derived from a system" that always enables the participants (employees) to express themselves. This result can never be achieved by leaders who tend to make long-winded statements.

The ability to remain eloquently silent is characterized by three skills. With the help of the following checklist, check whether and to what extent you already use these skills in your daily professional dealings.

Leadership is self-control. That is why leaders should concentrate on optimizing their own behavior—such as their communication skills—and enabling others to exercise their own self-leadership.

Table 11.1

The 3 Skills of Eloquent Silence		never	seldom	often	always
Ration your share of the conversation	I make sure that my speech is concise and focused (a maximum of three central statements)—I clarify these for myself before the meeting!				
	I do not repeat my arguments, but speak only to add new aspects and thoughts.				
	I work with imagery that is easy to remember (e.g. "Our success is rectangular" or "Our three stages should be . . .").				
Listen effectively	I listen attentively and make sure that I do not begin to formulate my response while the other person is still talking.				
	I deliberately gather statements, opinions, and appraisals from others in order to get the clearest possible picture.				
	I take notes and try to draw (with a mind map, for example) a complete picture of the views and aspects that come to light.				
Ask questions	I concentrate on genuinely understanding my counterpart and paying attention to how I "hear" what I already "knew".				
	I avoid valuations—even of statements and comments that criticize or question my wishes, or remind of different decisions.				
	I actively try to ensure that I understand the comments and contributions of others in the way they are intended by asking again.				

Note: The self-test questions for which your self-assessment falls in the "never" or "seldom" boxes highlight areas in which self-reflection, development, and change might be indicated.

Rule 12

Attempt to Orchestrate
Conflict with New Ideas

If it is true that smart leaders are continually training their employees, then their own open-mindedness regarding development and change is of major importance. Smart leadership is the effective organization of uncertainty and change. Leaders who allow the opportunities of the future to speak to them are in a position to design their own lives around curiosity, openness, and the ability to learn. In her book *This Is the Way It Is, But It Could be Different*, Swiss philosopher Helga Nowotny writes:

> Every question-answer exercise results in "more" than what was initially asked. These (material) left-overs often reveal new gaps in our understanding. If it is possible to ask big questions on the basis of small amounts of data, the difference between big and small disappears. . . . With the relativizing effect of multiple perspectives, partial appearances are the norm; the recurrence of similar assertions and bits of information can link everything with everything else." (Nowotny, 1999, p. 118)

The relative openness of the future casts doubt on previously assumed certainties. This is why effective leadership no longer relies solely on its own impressions, but must be aware of the risks that emerge from hanging on to old beliefs (see Rule 5). In summary, the key dimensions of future-oriented leadership can be summarized as in Table 12.1.

These dimensions are the starting points of future-oriented leadership and refer to the segmentation of what in practice translates to all the specific development activities—from the "involvement of the participants" to (strong) "strategic leadership"—and what they can mean in the workplace, in teams, and for the individual. Leaders who want to understand how their actions contribute to development should check the table above to see which aspects of development promotion they are already practicing and what requires additional work in the future.

Table 12.1   Dimensions and Starting Points of Future-oriented Leadership

Expansion	Leadership is not only about structures, organizational charts, responsibilities, and job descriptions. Such specifications tend to create inflexibility. A vibrant organization, in contrast, thrives on involvement and integration of employee potentials. Employees want to identify with the organizational objectives and processes. *Organizations consist of symbolic worlds.*
Evolution	When external factors are constantly changing, an organization cannot persist in rigid routines. For this reason, the appreciation of new things and the creative handling of innovation is essential for every kind of organizational development. *At the core, every organization is a fluid context of social interaction.*
Teambuilding	Organizations are not based on heroic management by one individual, but on the successful cooperation of many. To ensure the constructive cooperation of many people, it is essential they consider themselves as valuable and responsible. A focus on the employees and other resources is the essential basis for successful team/group development and appreciation is communicated through credible delegation of responsibility to others. *Organizations develop through successful cooperation.*
Perceived value	People don't want to simply perform a duty; they want to be a part of a significant undertaking. For this reason, the question "What general individual and social concerns do we address?" is vital to healthy organizational development. *Organizations thrive on the tangible value produced by their work.*
Interpretation	People interpret the world and the role they play in it. This is also true of their role in relation to organizations. Organizations must allow room for free interpretation and invite the employees to participate in the interpretation and re-interpretation of tasks and solutions. This allows development of both the individual's professional identity and an overarching organizational identity. *Organizations need room for interpretation.*
Coaching	Learning organizations are serious about feedback. They care how others see them and search for what may have been overlooked in their routines. Coaching is an important tool in helping leaders, colleagues, or individual teachers to systematically "organize" external views. *Learning organizations worry about their "blind spots".*
Communication	Formal and informal communications are the social material from which organizations develop. For this reason, it is important to provide "vessels" or mediums in which work-related communication and conflict resolution can take place and binding agreements made. This is an important part of organizational expression. *Organizations express themselves through the forms of their communication.*

Table 12.1   (Continued)

Unambiguous	The fluid nature of an organization requires a clear understanding of what steps are to be taken, and in which direction. Only when all participants know what is expected of them, can they be ready to commit themselves and find their position within the organization. Short-, middle-, or long-term plans are given substance by clear vision and guiding principles. *Organizations are built on the clarity of their goals and the reliability of their procedures.*
Leadership	Leaders still play a key, although different, role in the development of organizations. They must learn how not to lead and create complex organizations according to their own counsel, but rather to enable sustainable and dynamic change. Leaders are successful if an organization learns and develops. *Leadership is the enabling of capacity building and organizational learning.*
Networking	Organizations are constantly moving within a regional or organizational environment; resulting from relationships with entities such as stakeholders and potential partners. Networks link the organization to relevant outside interests and exploit the potential of possible inter-organizational cooperation and the distribution of resources. It allows each individual organization to do more than it could do alone. *Networked organizations open and exploit new perspectives.*

Rule 13

Practice Skills Development with Your Employees

Smart leaders lead their employees to achieve their own personal development goals. In doing so, a leader must ask about the areas in which employees would like to expand or improve. This is more specific than the overused question "Where do you want to be in five years?" When leaders lead with the future of the employees in mind, the system develops according to its potential and the "inner location from which the system acts" is shifted, as C. Otto Scharmer of the Massachusetts Institute of Technology writes (Scharmer, 2007, p. 380). In another passage, Scharmer and Käufer define learning "as an encounter with the self to be" and explain its significance to the smart leader (Scharmer and Käufer, 2011, p. 35 ff.):

> The challenges confronting executives today are characterized by high complexity, volatility, and far-reaching economic, ecological, and social change. . . . This means they face challenges that demand not only new technical, but also social and self-transformative skills—not only of the individual leader, but also as an organization and as an integrated system. (ibid. p. 35)

The leader who attempts to lead with a regard to the future of the employees inevitably will ask the question of what skill development is fundamentally possible. Leaders cannot answer this question in isolation. However, they can create an environment that encourages individual change and self-reflection. The opening question asking about the areas in which they would like to expand or improve not only confronts employees, but also offers them an opportunity to systematically reflect on it on their own. Smart leadership creates experts in the creation of a skills development context—a new element in the leadership debate.

Smart leaders lead "with an eye to the future" (Scharmer, 2007) by asking employees their "possible" skills and creating an enabling atmosphere where reflection and development of those skills are possible.

An employee at a large chemical company reports how she "stumbled over" the question of skills development:

> *Well, I have to admit that at first, I thought it was ridiculous: a new department head came from the United States, and instead of telling us what ideas he had for the future of the department, he started asking us what ideas we had. I can still remember that one of his questions was: "Why are you working here? What competences do you want to develop in your life, and how does the context in which you are working right now support that?"*
>
> *At the time, I only thought, "Doesn't he have any ideas of his own? It's easy for him to talk. I work here because they took me. And it's his job to tell me what I'll be doing in the future!" To make a long story short, our new department head eventually did tell us what topics he wanted to focus on in the near future and what goals he was pursuing or had been instructed to pursue. But he didn't share this with us until the third day of the so-called kick-off workshop. He spent the two days before that repeatedly asking us about our own ideas and got everyone to "show their colors."*
>
> *Now, this all sounds a bit harsh; what I want to say is that the processes he set in motion were truly moving. I would never have thought that was possible: even the skeptics in our department suddenly told us how they imagined their professional and private futures, and everyone was able to clearly articulate what they would like to "make of themselves" if given the chance. At the end of the second day, these skills-development posters were hanging all over the walls of the seminar room.*
>
> *And, I have to admit that it was quite impressive how Mr. Lorenz—that was the name of our new department head—was able to link his own projects to these plans. He didn't have a PowerPoint presentation; he just drew a picture of the individual potentials he had heard about over the past two days. So, at the end of the process, we all had something in common. And Mr. Lorenz said, "We'll discuss what this means for each of you in skills development sessions that I will conduct with each of you personally during the course of the next three weeks." I thought to myself, "Wow! That was really smart and smooth!"*

THE FOUR STEPS TO SKILLS DEVELOPMENT

Rather than a series of individual skills-development activities, the following four steps are more like functions. This means that some of the activities in an individual step may also be present or may cease to be useful, at a more advanced stage (adapted from Kossack, 2009, p. 58).

A skills-development dialog is a personnel-development conversation in which the leader (or personnel developer) goes through these four steps in a

Table 13.1

Steps or process functions	Activities
Orientation	• Make contact • Become acquainted (with a short presentation of your own portfolio) • Clarify roles (duties of others, etc.) • Framework conditions (time frame, perspectives) • State concerns (prioritization where required) Step 1: Agree on a goal
Explanation	• Explain current situation (context, background, changes) • Clarify future expectations • Discuss successes and experiences with previous approaches • Clarify procedures Step 2: Clarify duties (goal specification)
Development	• Develop new perspectives • Develop various possible solutions/courses of action • Discuss various consequences and evaluate alternative courses of action • Make decisions • Develop sub-goals Step 3: Plan specific measures
Outlook	• Record results • Secure transfer • Explain evaluation criteria or measures • Provide feedback and evaluate the conversation Step 4: Agree on future dialog steps to develop skills as required

one-on-one conversation. It is important that the highlighted steps are completed and documented. At the end of the conversation, both sides must be clear on what happens next, and what long-term goal needs the skill to be developed.

Rule 14

Promote Team Development

Today, personnel development strategies and personnel management experts rank team development as the number one concern. In order to take individual employees and form them into teams, leaders must take into account four different aspects of social interaction in their department or working group. These four aspects are shown in Table 14.1.

The combination of these two levels (relationship and technical) in an organization is often illustrated using the iceberg model, which is also known as the "Titanic phenomenon." The problem to be solved is more or less clear, but is it just the tip of an iceberg, with the rest unseen among the much larger flow of organizational life, often taking its destructive toll below the surface. Even when it seems outwardly fine, a project can be sunk by the underlying fears, attitudes, prejudices, and (negative) experiences of the team members.

During a school development project conducted over the course of a school day, participants formed groups whose task was to develop one of the five areas of change that had been identified as necessary for the "path to non-violent and humanistic schools." In the group that concentrated on "preventing violence," work never really got started. From the very beginning, two rival factions competed with each other: one wanted to intensify teacher presence in the schoolyard in order to permit immediate action in the event of every little conflict, while the other insisted on what it called the right to "relax and regenerate."

The discussions degenerated into personal attacks such as "All you care about is your own well-being!" or "Every school situation doesn't have to be a teacher issue!" The spokespersons for the two groups were from two different camps within the faculty. While the champion of allowing teachers to relax, a representative on the staff council, tried to give priority to the interests of the teachers, the champion of "presence in the schoolyard," who

59

Table 14.1

The four dimensions of team development— Self check: What about . . . ?			− −		+ +
Technical level	Goal orientation	Does the team have a clear focus on the goals? Are the main goals communicated and do all participants know what they are?			
	Task accomplishment	Is the accomplishment of tasks the main focus, or are there distractions? Are the participants noticeably committed to efficiency and effectiveness?			
Relationship level	Team cohesion	Is the team cooperative, mutually supportive, and loyal to the organization? Are conflicts kept in check and resolved internally without reducing synergy?			
	Assumption of responsibility	Do trust and delegation function within the team? Is the assumption of responsibility enabled and respected?			

was known as a dedicated and aspiring teacher, argued for fundamental change and improvements in teaching and school methods in almost every discussion. Everyone in the group quickly got the impression that a constellation had again emerged that they knew all too well and they didn't believe that they could effectively agree on anything in a goal-oriented fashion (Arnold and Arnold-Haecky, 2009, p. 128f).

This example illustrates that while a clear assignment and common goals are necessary, they do not ensure success. Instead, success is primarily driven by team cohesion and a culture of cooperation characterized by helpful, solution-oriented communication. The following rule is therefore fundamental to effective leadership: Leaders must deliberately build a culture of cooperation within the organization; just as they work to achieve goals and fulfill assignments, they must work to promote this culture.

THE TEAM-BUILDING PROCESS

A culture of cooperation is only one of the necessary steps for successful team development. Leaders should not expect everything to happen at once; it takes time for a group to become a team. This process is usually crisis-ridden and rife with disagreement and conflict. Only by successfully coping with crises can the group move on to the next level. W. Staehle promotes a proven four-phase process of group development that is also appropriate for team development.

Table 14.2 Phases of Group Development According to Tuckman

Phase	Group characterization	Task processing
1. Forming	Uncertainty, dependence on a leader, experimentation to discover what behavior is acceptable in a given situation.	Members define tasks, rules, and suitable methods.
2. Storming	Conflicts between subgroups, rebellion against the leader, polarization of opinions, rejection of group control over individuals.	Emotional refusal of task orientation.
3. Norming	Development of group cohesion, norms, mutual support, reduction or resolution of resistance and conflicts.	Open exchange of opinions and feelings, emergence of cooperation.
4. Performing	Resolution of interpersonal problems, emergence of a group structure that is functional for the accomplishment of tasks and role behavior that is flexible and functional.	Emergence of solutions, implementation of constructive task processing, full dedication of energy to the task (main working phase)

(Staehle, 1989, p. 256)

Rule 15

Create a Learning Organization

The term "learning organization" (Argyris and Schön, 2002) has become ubiquitous in today's corporate environment. There is hardly an organization that doesn't claim to be a learning organization. However, it is often a mere rhetorical makeover for business as usual. Such leaders have missed the radical nature of the concept. True learning organizations are characterized by a completely transformed method of cooperation and leadership.

A leader who wants his organization to learn must systematically eliminate all obstacles to learning: the constraints on employee motivation, courage, or willingness to change. Employees must feel that change is always possible and that the impulse and innovation to shape this change is up to them. Although still ultimately responsible for success, smart leaders realize that they can only guarantee success by caring about the development of their employees.

Smart leaders are responsible for creating learning spaces. Success is measured by the ability of leaders to promote and sustain individual movement, agility, commitment, and innovation.

In this context, appreciation and self-involvement are important. Learning organizations flourish in an environment where all participants clearly identify with the goals. Simultaneously reinforced through daily experience, they can be certain in the knowledge that their common action does not represent something fabricated somewhere else from a mix of tasks, responsibilities, job descriptions, and regulatory processes, but rather is something that they themselves can design and develop through cooperation. Learning organizations are characterized by transparent management and clear orientation, but also by an open-minded and participative management.

The manager of a software company related his experiences to his coach as follows:

*To be honest, I always have to control myself to keep from jumping in to control
and improve things down to the tiniest detail. This coaching process has made me
realize that such "micro-management" serves only my old images of leadership. It
hasn't been easy to realize that by doing that, I often create more confusion and
slow the processes down. Even more devastating is the distrust that I repeatedly
communicate with such behavior.*

*No wonder my team never really bought my talk about a learning organization.
Today, I would say that "an organization begins to learn when its leader begins to
relearn." Leaders need a new focus. They can no longer stare exclusively at their
products and at their key performance indicators like a snake staring at its prey.
Instead, they must look at the process of innovation. Meanwhile, I have adjusted to
the paradox: Now, I ensure that things are regularly questioned and new suggestions are sufficiently articulated.*

Gilbert Probst (1987) has compiled a list of recommendations for managing complex situations that effectively consists of creative suggestions for
systematically encouraging learning. This list shows that leadership must
focus less on avoiding and eliminating deficits, and more on recognizing
and eliminating systemic limitations to individual and team initiatives and
momentum.

Table 15.1   Systemic Leadership

Systemic Leadership Principles	
Principle	*Discussion*
Treat the system with respect.	See what is there! Withhold judgment! Show empathy! *Do not simply assume responsibility, but concern yourself with your own positive energy before approaching others, let alone intervening.*
Learn to deal with ambiguity, vagueness, and insecurity.	Be tolerant of ambiguity. *Remain suspicious of all problem-free proposals and one-dimensional explanations and attempts to describe causal relationships. Assume that everything could be and, in many cases, is completely different.*
Preserve and create opportunities.	Ask about alternatives. Use the system's resources. Tap into positive energy. *Recognize inertia, routines, complacency, and self-praise. There is nothing that cannot be improved, and different perspectives lead to different perceptions.*
Increase autonomy and integration.	Increase independence and personal responsibility. *Refrain from doing everything yourself—delegate responsibility. Before putting a rule into effect, ask yourself who participated in its development. If you cannot think of anyone, you have just developed a second-rate solution.*

Table 15.1 (Continued)

Systemic Leadership Principles	
Principle	*Discussion*
Exploit and promote the system's potential.	Develop self-control. *Avoid unnecessary involvement. Always ask yourself which inner image is driving your actions (once again) and make clear to yourself how little contact you have to the person you are speaking with in these moments.*
Define and solve problems.	Instead of looking for scapegoats, analyze the system. *Assigning blame paralyzes the synergy of cooperation. Even if you think you are certain, always try to identify and foster the positive potential of "at-fault" or "difficult" employees.*
Observe the levels and dimensions of creativity and management.	Support your team's development as a learning organization. *Concentrate!—like a scientist—on the big picture. Refrain from immediate reactions, but shift your reaction into the bigger context.*
Preserve flexibility and qualities of adaption and evolution.	Examine problems and solutions from different points of view. *Every question has numerous sides. Find out from what perspectives the important actors are judging events.*
Move from surviving to attaining viability and finally to development.	Learn to anticipate. Install early warning systems. *Introduce regular employee workshops or strategy debates about the future. Work with your employees in redefining your area of responsibility.*
Synchronize decisions and actions in the system with time-oriented systemic events.	Be flexible. *Not every question demands an immediate answer or even an immediate reaction. Always think your actions through, starting with the goal. Rely on the system's self-clarifying and self-healing powers and ensure that your own imagination does not lag behind the actual change (in evaluations, motives, and activities).*
Keep the process going.	*Avoid action for the sake of action. Do not initiate a process or something you cannot monitor. Restrict yourself to the management of core processes and keep track of them.*
There are no final solutions.	Solutions are dependent on time and situation. *Avoid inflexibility. Know how strongly you feel about certain solutions and be especially reserved in your discussions concerning them.*
Balance the extremes.	Avoid polarization. *Every time you face opposition, analyze the situation thoroughly and try out empathetic, appreciative, and integrative interpretations of the situation.*

(Italics expand on: Probst 1987, quotes from von Saldern 2010, p. 176)

Rule 16

Practice Capacity Building—Support Individual and Organizational Networking

Smart leaders measure their success by how well they are able to initiate, pool, and develop capacities. Effective leadership is therefore a networked activity that promotes self-direction of the system. At the same time, capacity building (cf. Eade, 1997) is defined as the deliberate combination of individual initiative, systematic development of human resources, and organizational development with the aim of improving the abilities of the system and its participants to successfully shape and optimize change.

In this context, Peter Senge has stated:

> . . . it is indeed possible to develop and internalize practical basic skills for a systems approach and a fundamental ability to reflect in the interests of developing a truly collective vision. . . . In other words, develop a somewhat less egotistical approach to your own clever ideas, which may not always be as effective as you think, and try to understand that there are good reasons for people in a complex system to have very, very different opinions about how to improve a situation. (Senge et al., 1996, p. 494)

Smart leadership not only sees the whole, but also makes an effort to recognize, link, and reinforce individual resources to aid in the development of system capacities. Such capacity building refers to the "creation of networks to strengthen social collaboration" (Horelli, 2003) and to encourage improvement (Stringer, 2008).

LEADERSHIP THROUGH NETWORKING

The creation and use of informal networks has recently been discussed, especially in international debates, as a way to stimulate, supervise, and support

67

the development of individuals, groups (teams), organizations, and regions. Smart leadership, according to the essential message of these discussions, is increasingly forced to shape social cooperation, which is not held together by rank and power, but through networks.

According to Manuel Castells's studies of the information society, a new staff structure is emerging based on each individual's position and opportunities within the network. Castells distinguishes between:

- the networkers, who create connections on their own initiative—for example, structures shared with other company departments—and navigate the network paths of the company;
- the networked, those who are online without deciding when, how, why, and with whom;
- the disconnected, employees who are bound to their specific tasks by non-interactive one-way orders. (Castells, 2004, p. 275)

This differentiation, according to Castells, results in the differentiation of corporate roles between the following types:

- the decision makers, who ultimately make the important decisions
- the participants, who are involved in the decision-making process
- the operators, who merely execute the decisions

Leaders who are interested in strengthening and developing the system's capacities must inspire, support, and promote networking, and also create space for participation and opportunities for collaboration among all network partners to maintain a dynamic spirit of self-direction.

LEADERS MODERATE OPERATIONAL
SELF-ORGANIZATION

The smart leader sees the need to move "from heroic leadership *in* the system to wise leadership *of* the system" (Doppler, 2009, p. 4)—a role that intentionally contributes to the development of a self-directing organization and corresponds to the following pattern:

(1) Listen in on the system to explore the organizational energy that is fundamentally present;
(2) Provide direction, depending on the situation, as necessary to open, connect, and bundle existing energy fields;
(3) Carefully observe and analyze the effect of this direction;

(4) Give the system enough time to respond, to test itself, or to intensify its own direction or to adjust;

(5) At the same time, by means of confrontational dialog, keep "forcing" those concerned to accept the requirements to take more individual responsibility and self-direction as is required in this style of leadership and to review their own actual behavior. (ibid, p. 5)

BASIS: NEW WAYS OF THINKING AND PERCEPTION

Change management researchers at the Massachusetts Institute of Technology assume that the unfamiliar can only emerge when leaders fundamentally change their thinking and consciousness.

All real change is grounded in new ways of thinking and perceiving. As Einstein said: "We can't solve a problem by using the same kind of thinking that created it." . . . A sustainable world, too, will only be possible by thinking differently. With nature and not machines as their inspiration, today's innovators are showing how to create a different future by learning how to see the larger systems of which they are part and to foster collaboration across every imaginable boundary. These core capabilities—seeing systems, collaboration across boundaries, and creating versus problem solving—form the foundation and, ultimately, the tools and methods for this shift in thinking. (Senge et al., 2008, p. 11)

Leadership works through the experience of others. That is why it is important for leaders to ask themselves how their behavior is perceived by their employees. Leaders cannot guarantee the effect they will have on others, but they can create the preconditions for development. Effective leadership also involves the continuing education opportunities for employees who show a readiness to advance. This trend embraces all levels of the enterprise. For instance, enterprises expect even candidates for high-level technical and leadership positions to demonstrate a "willingness to grow" (Institut der Deutschen Wirtschaft, 2011a, p. 5).

Rule 17

Be a Friend to the Unexpected

People live by safe expectations: the result and the expression of our cognitive and emotional development. If we study the work of Swiss developmental psychologist Jean Piaget (1896–1980), we see that perception templates, terms, and actions, once acquired, assist us in orienting to new situations. We can only relate to the new situation with the help of our old experiences, a process that makes us unintentionally assume that the new will mirror the old.

To a certain extent, this explains why the unexpected only appears when we consciously break away from the usual terms, models, and concepts that determine our thoughts. Jean Piaget referred to the "equilibrium of the consciousness" as the effort of every person to keep experiences, interpretive patterns, and strategies in balance: "As different as the goals of intention and action may be, the subject always tries to avoid inconsistencies and tends toward specific forms of balance without ultimately achieving them" (Piaget, 1975, p. 170; von Glaserfeld, 2011, p. 199).

The tendency of people to search for consistency and balance between retention and change helps us to understand why unexpected developments are sometimes overlooked or even ignored, and why people tend to continue with their current plans even when the signs of the times have already changed. Companies that have proven themselves able to handle surprises and changing circumstances remarkably successfully have done so by creating special precautions that help them to act and react attentively and flexibly. Karl E. Weich and Kathleen M. Scutcliffe of the University of Michigan attribute the success of those companies to the following:

> . . . they do an extraordinarily good job of developing different forms of awareness
> and thereby always have an eye on what is happening. They regularly update their
> ideas of events and do not remain entrenched in old categories of thinking or

half-baked interpretations of the outside conditions which confront them. (Weick
and Scutcliffe, 2010, S. VIII)

On the basis of their analysis of how companies learn from extreme situations, they are developing a complex self-test to assess awareness within the
company. The key question in this assessment is, "Do you have the ability
to flexibly deliver top performance?" (ibid, p. 87). To help answer this question, they systematically and self-critically examine the following areas:

- Assessment of company awareness
- Tendency towards a careless attitude
- Areas requiring specific attention
- Focus on errors
- Aversion to simplification
- Sensitivity to operating processes
- Pursuit of flexibility
- Respect for specialist knowledge and abilities (ibid, p. 91ff).

Selected items from the self-test shown in Table 17.1 should help the
leader to get a clear picture of the company's openness to change and its
ability to recognize change early and to manage it productively.

These items do not provide a complete picture of adaptive abilities of
individuals, or entire teams. However, they do allow leaders to readjust their
focus on factors that are thought to be relevant for success. Smart leaders can
learn how to equip themselves and their teams to deal with the unexpected.
They also broaden the view of present situational requirements by means of a
strategic approach "from the future" (Scharmer, 2007). This forward-looking
orientation is more than a new buzzword; it shakes previous leadership and
learning concepts to their very core.

The head of an international department expressed the following:

*We have increasingly distanced ourselves from the idea that we must prepare our
employees for the future by offering them further training. To be honest, we don't
really know what the future holds; we have only our own ideas of it. So, we have
decided to take a different path: we prepare our people to deal with the unexpected
and strengthen their ability to adjust to the future when it arrives.*

Table 17.1 Self-assessment of the Ability to Deal with the Unexpected

Aspects of the ability to deal with the unexpected		− −	−	+	+ +
Awareness	Leaders pay as much attention to managing the unexpected as to achieving official business objectives				
	We invest time and effort into determining whether our actions could in any way harm our environment, customers, shareholders, or others involved				
Carelessness	The situations, problems, or questions we have are the same every day				
	There is little leeway in decisions and operations to react immediately if unexpected problems occur				
Need for attention	Events are followed immediately by feedback and information that can be effortlessly verified				
	There are many opportunities to improvise if something goes wrong				
Attention to Mistakes	Mistakes are not held against those who make them				
	Leaders ask about possible bad news of their own accord				
Interpretations	We are concerned with questioning the status quo				
	The employees are encouraged to express different views of the world				
Sensitivity	Leaders gladly fill in for others whenever necessary				
	The employees always seek feedback that might reveal faulty processes				
Flexibility	Our organization explicitly concerns itself with fostering the skills and knowledge of its employees				
	Colleagues are known for their ability to use their knowledge in new ways				

(Adapted from: Weick/Sutcliff 2010, p. 91 ff.)

Rule 18

Avoid Elaborate PowerPoint Presentations

PowerPoint is no longer "hot" in a leadership context according to the *Frankfurter Allgemeine* newspaper. The article states that a transition from Power-Point has already begun in numerous enterprises. The reason? PowerPoint relies too heavily on cinematic effects, and the long-term effectiveness of such laboriously designed slides is alarmingly limited. According to the article,

> Throughout the world, this drama repeats itself every day in office buildings, hotels, and convention halls. Legions of buzzwords and diagrams on carefully designed PowerPoint slides bearing company logos appear on screens for hours on end, and with each new slide, more and more of the audience tunes out. It is no consolation that a printed version is occasionally distributed at the end of such presentations. The copies will only collect dust, unopened, on some shelf. Malicious tongues even claim that the less someone has to say, the more extensive the PowerPoint will be.
>
> However, a gradual process of rethinking has begun—even in the consulting industry, which has traditionally been particularly enthusiastic about PowerPoint. "Consultants certainly do themselves no favors when they entrench themselves behind slides during public presentations. We must stop that," as Frank Mattern, head McKinsey-Germany, recently said. (Löhr, 2010, p. 20)

PowerPoint presentations convey hidden messages that reflect an outmoded top-down leadership style. These messages do not fit in with the systemic concerns of smart leaders.

This criticism of PowerPoint presentations is highly justified because they are good vehicles for announcing but not for discovering or integrating diverse initiatives. An excessive or too-perfect presentation violates the spirit of smart leadership in six ways:

Table 18.1

Unintended consequences of a perfect PowerPoint presentation	Hidden message to the audience
Dull	"The next few minutes will focus on the subject matter, not your thoughts."
Inflexible	"Everything has been so well thought out and prepared that it is beyond questioning, comments, or criticism."
Elitist	"My terrific presentation shows that I really know more about this topic than you or anyone else."
Discourages boldness	"This presentation is so slick and convincing that I don't dare to interrupt the speaker."
Undesired interest	"Please don't interrupt—just listen! I consider every word to be a disturbance!"
Closed	"The presentation is all thought out, and I am merely sharing it with you. Don't get the idea that you might have anything to add."
Exhaustive	"You are no match for me; you can see that I have prepared thoroughly."

After a half-hour of looking at more than thirty PowerPoint slides, a colleague finally raised her hand and asked, "I'd like to know whether you intend to ask us any questions." When she noticed the speaker's thunderstruck reaction, she explained, "Since the fifth diagram, I have had the impression that you already know everything and that you only want to instruct or at least, inform us. If that is the case, you could have simply mailed us your views. That's why I asked whether you have questions for us."

This public questioning of the value of the presentation stunned the speaker and, unable to respond in any other way, he awkwardly replied, "I guess you are right: I assumed that I had been asked to present my insights, thoughts, and conclusions. If you have any questions, I will try to answer them and explain them in more detail, but I don't know whether that is what you wanted to hear." My colleague responded sarcastically, "Well, I did not come here to be lectured to like a schoolgirl. I had thought, someone is coming who is interested in discussing his ideas with people who have practical experience, in order to learn as well, but you act as if you already know everything and are graciously sharing your knowledge with us. My time is too valuable to be wasted like this. I haven't been a schoolgirl in twenty-five years!"

It is rare that such feelings are so expressed in a truly open forum. Normally, the listeners accept their fate, which they do not find too difficult, as they are strongly influenced by the past experience of the top-down learning culture to which such presentations belong. They are accustomed to situations in which they are instructed by others. Protests against top-down instruction are indeed rare. The normal reaction is to withdraw and feel detached.

Smart leadership relies on involvement and participation. To this end, effective leaders give no presentations, but interweave their own requirements, thoughts, and decisions with the perspectives of others. They avoid lengthy monologs and rely instead on dialog.

However, according to Martin Buber (1878–1965), dialog means nothing other than "accommodating the partner" (Buber, 2002, p. 293). The substance of the thoughts changes when the partner has the chance to speak. They are no longer finished constructs, prefabricated, communicated, and visualized, but more like invitations to discussion. They solicit more open concepts, instead of "selling" a finished construct.

The leader who decides ahead of time, goes so far as to finalize an issue, or pursues a linear approach before discussing it not only assumes there is only one possible way to understand the material; that leader also passes up the chance to intertwine his or her views with the possibilities presented by the audience. An effective leader presents questions that can lead to comments, estimations, and remarks on the part of the audience.

In the future, use your presentations to develop a consensus.

Table 18.2

The six steps to dialog	Questions
D emonstrate	What do you think of these questions on the topic? Which ones are missing?
I nform	Is this information correct? What does it mean?
A malgamate	Which additional aspects, pieces of information, or questions are relevant?
L et go	How does my approach need to be changed?
O ffer	What steps would you use to approach this topic?
G ratify	How can we integrate and value the results?

Rule 19

Learn to Distrust Yourself—The More Confident and Decisive Your Actions, the More You Should Distrust Them

Leaders can only perceive the world of their employees through the prism of their own experience. In situations involving conflict or requiring a decision, they will "act as their own feelings allow" (Arnold, 2009b) and only with some difficulty can they take in a new and accurate view of the present situation.

The continuous need to question their own certainties is the difficult challenge many managers fail to master. In this context, the American economist Peter Drucker (1909–2005) knew that "Few leaders realize that they must lead only one person, namely themselves" (Joka, 2002, p. 19).

What can smart leaders do to break out of this cycle of measured expectations? The cycle often leads them to see themselves again in the employees who are going through a similar situation. The older and more "experienced" the leaders get, the more they realize their own tendency to remain true to their own viewpoint. It is this being a prisoner of one's own certainty that the well-known professor of leadership development, Manfred Kets de Vries, speaks about as he describes the inner drama:

> The interface of our motivational needs with environmental factors (especially human factors, in the form of caregivers, siblings, teachers, and other important figures) defines our essential uniqueness. The mental schemas that are the outcome of this interface are then carried within us for the rest of our lives, guiding our subsequent relationships with others, and relationships help us make sense of all aspects of reality, serve as the standard by which we judge what we see and decide what we want, and govern our motivations and actions. These representations become the operational code that determines how we act and react in our daily lives, whether at home, at play, or at work. (Kets de Vries, 2006, p. 12)

It controls me? It leads me? Yes!

People, in a way, are not absolute masters of their own ships because whatever they think, feel, and do is tied to their "inner representations." For this reason, neuroscientist Gerald Hüther challenges us to try to be led "not by our previous interpretations, but by our imaginations" (cf. Hüther, 2011, p. 14). We tend to see in a certain situation only what our own experience lets us see. In any situation, our conscious programming, images, and feelings kick in to give us that "safety" of the "way things are."

Rarely from this "self-certainty", can any rational—let alone "scientific"—examination of the facts and conditions take place. Rather, the outcome is the result of some counterbalance that we carry within us that sometimes misleads us. Furthermore, there seems to be a paradoxical regularity in the patterns of thought, the effect of which can be minimized if the leader considers the following rule: Our thoughts, feelings, and actions assert themselves with ever more certainty when older, deeper experience is involved. Therefore, recognize repetition and avoid emotionalized certainties.

We are literally possessed by what we think or feel to be certain, but with this certainty we are more connected to ourselves than with the motivations, intentions, and reasons of those with whom we are speaking. The mechanism of "the more certain, the more personal" leads the American therapist Steve de Shazer (1940–2005) to prescribe: "If you have an interpretation, take an aspirin, sit quietly in a corner, and wait until the interpretation is over" (Varga von Kibéd, 2008, p. 14)—a challenge that encourages skepticism of one's own beliefs, an approach that may also open up a path to the system, in other words, to the other actors with their own "certainties," which may consist of contradictory evaluations, perceptions, and positions.

Table 19.1

"Take an Aspirin" 7-Steps to access your own interpretations and beliefs (A S P I R I N)	
First step: Awareness	Before your own impressions solidify and unduly influence your perception and reaction, remind yourself that you already carried the potential of these experiences, interpretive patterns, and routines with you before you met the other party to the conversation.
Second step: Self-perception	Slow down your perception and thoughts and try to observe your own observation. Ask yourself what features of your observations and interpretations remind you of yourself. Especially in conflict situations, ask yourself in what aspects are you remaining "true" to yourself.
Third step: Package the problem focus	Whenever you rashly and willingly step into the void or allow yourself to become tied down in the discovery of problems, note how you fall into the *trance of problem solving*. Realize that a problem can also be a solution—if an incomplete one—and intentionally make your contributions in a way that sounds like a search for explanations and not for something/someone to blame for the problem.
Fourth step: Innovation	Embrace difference and let yourself be surprised with different, unusual explanations and ideas, or allow yourself to be stumped. React with patience and show an appreciative response to *new readings of familiar topics* and show yourself as disturbed with an unsettled reaction to *old versions of new topics*.
Fifth step: Retrogrades	Practice the art of reversing "final judgments" and pronouncements. If you have alienated, hurt, or even "rejected" someone, approach them again and again – better one time too many than one time too few. Consider: your position as the superior is always the stronger, so you can afford to surprise others with candor, self-criticism, and flexibility.
Sixth step: Interviews	Leaders cannot ultimately know what others think, feel, suspect, or fear. The ability to listen and ask questions is a significant dimension of smart leadership. Visit regularly with employees at their workplaces and purposefully ask what motivates them.
Seventh step: New beginning	The leaders role is to explore new paths, not guard traditional ones. Great importance is placed on the visionary power and prudence of the leader. They have to "discover" new truths (opportunities) for the organization without immediately embracing them. Furthermore, they cannot rely on tradition or limit themselves to ensuring that nobody leaves the familiar path. Instead, always look for opportunities and imagine the future of the system!

Rule 20

Acknowledge Your Inner Images of Leadership and Loyalty

Our thoughts, feelings, and actions are determined by the images and ideas we have acquired in the past. In this context, the Bremen brain researcher Gerhard Roth refers to the influence of early childhood experiences in the development of personality:

> There has been much controversy about the actual effect of the first few years of life on the development of personality. While a few psychologists and pedagogues assign no special meaning to early childhood experiences and assume a constant malleability of human personality, the majority have come to the conclusion that the first three to five years, and, to a lesser extent puberty, have a significant influence on later life, particularly as concerns temperament. (Roth, 2011, p. 68)

These early influences on temperament are directly activated in situations in which we are emotionally challenged, specifically situations that have to deal with recognition ("How do others see me?"), dependence ("Who can tell me what I am supposed to do?"), attention ("Who cares about me?"), and inadequacy ("What can I really change?"). Leaders must learn "to observe themselves internally as they face these situations. What feelings are activated when the expected attention is not received or when we feel ourselves to be ineffectual in our efforts?" (Arnold, 2011, p. 18).

Smart leaders must be conscious of the specific forms taken by their feelings about the world. They must have developed an understanding of how their own perceptions affect their own, but also, unavoidably, the perceptions, judgments, and management actions of others and mislead them into being unfair to the other. The effective leaders comprehend these fragile substances from which our beliefs are formed and have developed mechanisms for expressing their own impressions with reserve.

The excerpt below reflects the story of a coach who succeeded in instigating a reflective change in someone who had maneuvered themselves onto the sidelines as a result of having a history of conflict with the supervisor. This changed not only the way of viewing things, but also the topic that dominated the focus:

> *When I look back, it becomes clear to me that I have confused something. I have always fought against my supervisors with an unbelievable stubbornness. I had nothing good to say about my last boss and discredited him in conversations with colleagues. Whenever he assigned me something or started a project, I felt immediately that I was against it—without opening my mind in the slightest to the details or his intentions.*
>
> *In retrospect, I regret it and I am just beginning to realize what the devil had gotten into me. It was a feeling that colored my view of anyone who had a position of authority over me. I felt somehow that I was taken for granted and kept stumbling into stubborn battles to be appreciated and noticed. I made myself laughable because I pretended to be something that I'm not. How often have I pretended to be the boss myself while I was away overseas! Now, as I begin to gradually realize all this, I deeply regret it.*
>
> *I see in retrospect that my bosses were really all very competent, patient, and personable types who were prepared—as difficult as I often made myself—to accept me as I was. I had to reach the age of fifty-eight before I realized what kind of personal program I was running and expecting others to accept.*

Such reflective movements characterize the path to effective leadership. The path is one of applied knowledge theory (Arnold, 2011), which encourages leaders to step back from their battles over the facts and observe from a distance why they struggle in the ways they do. In this way, they can learn to understand the deeply ingrained reasons for their own behavior, and to identify what drives their personality, "their unconscious self" as Roth expresses it (Roth, 2007, p. 274).

Self-reflective learning is difficult because the subject has subtle mechanisms of self-deception to hold onto his or her "certainties." The systems researcher Fritz B. Simon speaks in this context of "the art of not learning" (Simon, 2002)—a power that works in the background and causes the individual to believe it is the world of others, not one's own manner of observation, that is responsible for the complications that require some counter-response.

However, it is possible to identify one's own programs of interpreting and feeling (Arnold, 2008, p. 20ff) by ruthlessly retracing the tracks of one's own thoughts, feelings, and actions. The following questions can assist in this effort. Where the answers lie in the areas—further clarification and learning processes would be helpful on the path to smart leadership.

Table 20.1

Identifying your programs of interpretation and feeling		− −	−	+	+ +
Dealing with the need for recognition	At an early age, I experienced (from my parents) true recognition and knew who I was and what I could do.				
	I have been able to develop a clear feeling of belonging and safety.				
	No one has ever accused me of being concerned with myself instead of the matter at hand.				
Dealing with dependence	I was always able to experience dependent phases in my life (as a child, a student, an employee) appropriately and not as threatening or limiting.				
	I have never vehemently rebelled against dependence or attempted to free myself from it by means of radical action.				
	Seen from the other side: the people whom I lead do not feel themselves to be dependent, but participatory.				
Dealing with the need for attention	I have learned to simply receive attention without having to earn it.				
	I can turn my attention to myself, and there are a number of people who appreciate my ability to be in relationship with them.				
	I remain in contact with all my employees equally and do not isolate myself within groups ("leadership circles")				
Dealing with inadequacy	I am satisfied with what I have been able to achieve in my life and have learned that what one achieves is what one has "earned" in life.				
	I never feel that I am a victim of misunderstanding of deplorable circumstances in professional or private contexts.				
	I have the certain feeling that others also see in me what I see in myself.				

Rule 21

Analyze Your Attitudes and Your Motives

Leaders are people who have achieved their positions in competition with others. This implies that powerful personal motives have made leaders what they are. To truly understand leadership and leaders, it is necessary to understand what motivates them to seek positions of power. Leaders usually have an inner drive to make external change: leaders drive projects forward, make decisions, and take responsibility—usually driven by a self-motivated claim to authority and influence whose true source often remains hidden even from the leaders.

Smart leaders question the sources and patterns of their own attitudes and motivations. They ask themselves what it is that drives them and if their attitude and motivation bring them closer to others. In other words, closer to the problems, needs, and decision requirements of the moment, for which I have assumed responsibility.

In a leadership seminar, the following dialog took place between several participants:

> *"In my opinion, leadership is essentially a service to the people for whom one bears responsibility. I feel responsible for guaranteeing their jobs with my decisions because I successfully open up future opportunities (such as markets and ideas for products)." Another participant countered, "For me, leadership is a job: I use objective criteria for my decisions. I think it is exaggerated and unfair to make me responsible for how the markets develop." A critical voice then issued a frontal attack on both of them: "I think you are fooling yourselves, and in my opinion, you both work according to the principle, 'whatever is good for me is good for the company'! Do you really care how your employees are doing, how they feel, how they see their future, or what their wishes and needs are?"*

This sharp comment caused a discussion that focused on finding the attitudes and motives leaders can adopt to portray, justify, and legitimize their actions. Four general types of leader and motivation emerged:

Table 21.1

Behavior style	"Inner voices"	Subconscious drivers	Unintended consequences
Ethically oriented leadership	"I have to do good things and give them purpose."	"My behavior and my person are worthless unless I am noticeably doing good."	Danger of idealizing leadership by ignoring the necessity and legitimacy of conflict.
Fact oriented leadership	"I am only concerned with the facts; I am not emotionally involved or committed."	"If you do not remain objective, you will be sucked in."	Danger of a lack of relationships, being distant from others, and not getting critical information through lack of involvement.
Socially oriented leadership	"The only thing that counts is creating connections and bonds between people."	"You are nothing unless you bring about cooperation and consensus."	Danger of overemphasizing relationships while overlooking the fact that they cannot develop independently of the task.
Egocentric leadership	"I am destined to show what needs to be done and to lead the way."	"If you allow yourself to be questioned, you are nothing."	Danger of a narcissistically confusing objectivity with one's own desires.

The art of good leadership is characterized by the presence of leaders who have gained insights into their own motives. Good leaders know of the inner voices they hear when making decisions and resolving conflict, and they have strategies to avoid or compensate for the unintended consequences that follow when they judge, act, or decide "from the gut."

Smart leaders are familiar with the inner voices of leadership and have strategies and techniques to minimize or compensate for their influence.

Often, these inner voices have been recorded in early childhood, and avoidance or compensation for their effects is essential because of how deeply they are now anchored in the leader's perceptions. Leadership psychologist Manfred Kets de Vries says, "Greater self-awareness is the first step toward becoming a more effective leader" (Kets de Vries, 2006, p. 192).

This self-awareness cannot develop through cognitive learning alone. The exercising of personal interests and behavioral patterns can scarcely be overcome by insightful views or good intentions. What is required is an extensive phase (in the context of a coaching) during which behavior without—or with other—inner voices is practiced and "tolerated."

Table 21.2

Unintended consequences	Avoidance strategies	Compensatory strategies
Ethically oriented leadership: Danger of idealizing leadership by ignoring the necessity and legitimacy of conflict.	Development of questioning style of leadership: Seek other assessments and perceptions and develop your own opinion in a discourse without imposing it.	Leaders occasionally consider themselves to be victims of "unjust" or even "thankless" actions. *Remember: the victim must return to the table so that the contact does not die.*
Target-oriented leadership: Danger of a lack of relationships, being distant from others, and not getting critical information through lack of involvement.	Team-developing leadership: Consciously keep an eye on the group process and the moods and needs of the actors and discuss them under supervision, if necessary	Leadership without relationships often comes across as arrogant and overbearing. *Remember: show interest in the personal concerns of colleagues.*
Socially oriented leadership: Danger of overemphasizing relationships while overlooking the fact that they cannot develop independently of the task.	Standard-oriented leadership: Act with transparent target orientations, target agreements, key performance indicators, and timelines.	Leaders sometimes have a hard time expressing and imposing clear requirements in "fraternization contexts". *Remember: leadership also requires a clear definition of responsibilities.*
Egocentric leadership: Danger of a narcissistically confusing objectivity with one's own desires.	Self-reflective leadership: Leadership fundamentally requires reflective phases during which the leader can be self-critical of what is of actual importance.	Leaders often have insufficient time to thoroughly think through and track down problems, conflicts, and decisions. *Remember: leadership also requires phases of reflection.*

Rule 22

Make an Attempt at More Elegant Communication

Humans have been trying for a long time to understand and improve human communication. Several promising models of communication were in fact developed, even though they ultimately proved too general and were of little use. Some of these models came from information technology, which saw communication merely as the process of transferring information. It was assumed that the quality of this process—that is to say the quality of communication—was dependent only on the encoding by the sender, the suitability of the broadcast channel, and the decoding competences of the receiver (see Simon, 2004, p. 17).

Although these technical descriptions proved insufficient for describing complex human communication, they still influence our thoughts and behavior in communicative situations, and most leaders have heard of the content and relationship levels of human communication (Watzlawick et al., 1974), or the "four ears" with which we hear and the "four tongues" with which we speak (Schulz von Thun, 1990).

"Why don't you understand? How often do I have to tell you?" we ask, speaking louder and articulating more clearly, as if that makes the message easier to understand. Sometimes we are even upset at the incomprehension and the dull-wittedness of the person to whom we are speaking. We might even shout, "What! Am I speaking Chinese?" or "You just don't get it!"

Then, we become disappointed, annoyed, offended, or bewildered and stuck in our—justified or merely self-satisfying—certainty, which we announce, convey, or disguise in an appeal . . . not even noticing how antiquated our behavior is in terms of communication theory. It's the Stone Age standard of the one-dimensional communication of the "I told you so!"

Gerhard Roth and Monika Lück describe in an article on the "Neurobio-logical Basis of the Transmission of Knowledge in Training," the basic prob-lem of communication as follows:

> Why is the transmission of knowledge often so unsuccessful? One major reason is the misconception that this process is basically the transportation of information from the teacher's or trainer's head to the listeners' heads. If that were the case, effective teaching and learning would simply be a matter of the acoustics of commu-nication—the teacher would only have to speak loudly and clearly enough, and the listeners would just have to listen closely. . . . However, this is an illusion, although an understandable one. What the speaker or writer produces and what reaches the listener's ear and the reader's eye is merely physical events (acoustic pressure on the ears, arrangements of dark lines on a light background for the eyes), which do not have any meaning as such. Instead, the meaning is created in a highly subjective and individual way in the minds or the brains of the listener. . . . In order to give meaning to spoken or written words and clauses, the receiver's brain must command corresponding previous knowledge. Contexts must be present to give the symbols meaning. Meaning cannot be transmitted directly from the teacher to the learner at all; it must be constructed by the learner's brain. (Roth and Lück, 2010, p. 40)

These discussions make it very clear that "meanings must be constructed" (ibid) and cannot be "directed" or "instructed." If we want to accomplish anything with our "announcements," counseling sessions, or instructions, we must try to improve our communicative patterns rather than trying to perfect our input. Effective communication thrives on communicational elegance. The following are ten characteristics of elegant speech (adapted from Arnold, 2010):

Rule 1: Disentangle yourself from the assumption that the purpose of commu-nication is only for the transmission of messages and knowledge, and observe how you (and others) participate in social events through communication and strive for differentiation in your communication.

Those who succeed in seeing communication in this new way—as the material of which society is made—will have no trouble accepting that under-standing is the rare exception and misunderstanding is the norm.

Rule 2: If you want to communicate, present, or explain something, solicit questions. Avoid assertive or judgmental speech, even if the facts of the situa-tion appear to be clear.

To communicate effectively, we must learn to communicate "from the other's perspective," meaning that we have to understand other ways of per-ceiving, understanding, and learning. This can only be achieved through close observation and the discovery of how the other is approaching the communi-cation and what inner images and difficulties there may be.

Rule 3: Avoid the appeal—overt as well as covert; instead, suggest or invite!

There is no guarantee that your pleas will be received the way you intended them. The meanings attributed to a tasking or messages are always interrupted by a complex network of subjective experiences, associations, and individual intentions and questions. The message arrives as the receiver constructs it.

Rule 4: Do not try to convince others, but develop an interest in their diversity. Get used to dealing with the ambiguity of that which seems so clear to you.

Rule 5: Do not succumb to the illusion of communication. Coexistence and cooperation are made up not only of consent, but also of dissent. Practice dealing with dissent.

Rule 6: Develop a feeling for the power of traditions and social norms in the context of your communication.

Rule 7: Pay attention to how the person you are speaking to wants to be perceived in his communication.

Rule 8: Pay attention to the way you yourself appear in your communication, develop an ear for feedback, and consider the unintended risks and consequences of your style on results-oriented communication.

Rule 9: Practice meta-communication.

Rule 10: Create space in which to follow up and self-reflect.

Rule 23

Redefine "Difficult" Colleagues and Practice Your Emergence View

New theories about change management developed at the Massachusetts Institute of Technology reinforce the view of change as intransitive, not transitive. In other words, change has lost its object to a certain extent. The word "change" no longer describes an action by which a subject changes an object; instead, it describes a process during which the observing and judging subject itself changes.

The basis of this intransitive access to change originates in the theory of knowledge and the view of things that suggests smart leaders should no longer concentrate on the changing context or the context to be changed. Instead, they must focus on their own observations and how they reached their judgments, staying well aware of the fact that people want to remain true to their observations. We prefer to proceed for the umpteenth time with the familiar interactions, crises, or separations over making these, our perceptions, part of the problem.

"Do you mean to tell me that I am creating my 'difficult' employee myself? My colleagues also think that Mr. Schubert is hard to work with!" said an enraged executive in discussing this mechanism during a workshop. "I can tell him whatever I want, but he usually understands it wrong or not at all." A colleague added: "Mr. Schubert doesn't even have a chance in our team anymore. Everyone watches him, waiting to see what he will fail to understand next. Sometimes I have the impression that the poor man can do what he will and it won't make any difference—he's been labeled." One of the coaches added, "Yes, that is an interesting question: how does your team let this colleague's presence emerge? Perhaps we should all take some time to practice the 'EMERGENCE view' together."

The emergence view is a holistic observation of the other person that employs two types of views simultaneously: an introspective analysis ("How

95

do I routinely look at 'difficult' employees and how long have I been doing this?") and a view to the development potential ("What am I missing and why?").

Smart leadership is based largely on the ability of the leader to spot the emergence of potential. The emergence view is constantly asking the question "What experiences are pushing their way into my judgments?" Search for the deep-rooted cognitive subroutines that form perceptions and try to account for the distortions that might affect the perception of another person and, subsequently, affect decisions regarding this person. This, in effect, allows the other person to change (i.e., to "emerge" in a different light).

The emergence view is a deliberate search not only for the other person, but also for the internal processes leaders use to shape their perceptions. It immediately challenges certainties and allows the familiar to take on a new character.

Use the self-check in Table 23.1 to determine your own emergence view skills.

Leaders who practice the emergence view seem to deliberate and delay judgment. As Peter Senge and others would say, they have lost their "voice of judgment." They are then capable of following the advice of Senge and others who have determined,

> In practice, suspension requires patience and the willingness not to impose pre-established frameworks or mental models on what we are seeing. If we can simply observe without forming conclusions as to what our observations mean and allow ourselves to sit with all the seemingly unrelated bits and pieces of information we see, fresh ways to understand a situation can eventually emerge. (Senge et al., 2005, p. 31)

The point of the emergence view is all about the leader presenting a less judgmental attitude that is also less certain and more questioning. Of course, it will not eliminate all difficulties, and there will still be those who stand in the way, refuse to cooperate, or even sabotage the leader.

However, the following is also true: Leaders who master the emergence view spare themselves and others from hasty judgments and endless repetitions of the same experience (i.e., "I always have similar problems occurring at regular intervals."), which allows them to refocus on other aspects of the other person. In this way, the nature of those relationships can change and true leadership becomes possible.

Table 23.1

How good is my emergence view?		− −	−	+	+ +
Out with the old	I am conscious of "inherited burdens" (old experiences, images, etc.) on my thoughts, feelings, and actions and have found a way to ensure that they seldom interfere and blur my vision				
Break the pattern	I am able to consciously interrupt my own pattern (spontaneous judgment, impulsive action, etc.) and to react in a completely different manner than I myself had expected				
Less emotional	I am able to recognize when my feelings are beginning to dictate my judgment and actions and I can consciously go into a "no response" mode and allow a cool off period.				
Ritualized reactions	I have developed fixed routines to distance myself from the influence of my own emotions and experiences as well as from those of others				
Counter proposals	I am able to develop completely different explanations and impressions of the behavior of the other person than those that come to me spontaneously				
Expect expectations	I try to expect the expectations of others and by reflecting on the reciprocal nature, I can free myself of them.				
New thinking	If calm and composed, I can arrive at a new construction of what I had originally expected or feared.				
Grant second chances	I can forgive and develop renewed confidence in the other person because I have learned to mistrust my own images and suppress the power they have over me.				

Rule 24

Exercise Change Management through Self-Transformation

Self-transformation is not a call for self-reproach or a sign of retreat from opposition, conflicts, or intrigues. Rather, self-transformation is the only possible way to affect change in social relationships that must be maintained or cannot be avoided. We are too often unwilling to accept the simple fact that it is difficult, if not impossible, to change others. In the conflicts of our everyday lives, we keep trying to present our points of view in order to convince others to believe us or to accept our ideas. By contrast, we know that communication and brain researchers unanimously agree that such targeted intervention and comprehension are not truly attainable.

What consequences emerge for daily professional life from the futility of intervention and understanding?

During a coaching session, a young department manager exclaimed,

> *"I have come to accept that my employees tend to understand me in the way they do—you could also say, the way they want to. I've had some good experiences by not getting upset if someone doesn't follow my instructions or takes a different approach than I told them to. At first, I was against these 'arbitrary acts', but I have come to realize that I have to take a different approach: I communicate outcomes; specifically, I define what I expect in numbers whenever possible, how much and when. I refrain from providing any directions as to the how-to process.*
>
> *In my opinion, this is the art of leadership: when you realize that something isn't working, for God's sake, don't try even harder to keep doing things the old way, but try to change yourself or your style of leadership. As I've already mentioned, I've had some good experiences with key performance indicators because they are precise, they can only be understood for what they are, and you really feel much better.*

During this transformation, I'll be honest, I had to overcome my urge to supervise my employees because I had always believed that people are only

99

able to carry out their task effectively if told how to do it and are supervised closely to ensure that they do the tasks the way they are told. This fixation was very exhausting and ever since I was internally able to detach myself from it and change my leadership style, I have felt much better—and so have my employees, I think."

As this example clearly illustrates, self-transformation is not the result of the unilateral assignment of blame, but rather, an internal transformation can be a way to effect a change in others. If people do not feel compelled to act according to expectations, they are more likely to decide on their own how to best approach a challenge. The prerequisite for leaders in encouraging such self-transformation in others is to be smart enough to develop a leadership style laid out on the criteria for success and not on the basis of their own expectations of how leadership should be projected and respected.

Smart leadership means repeatedly evaluating or balancing the forms of directives, frameworks, and interventions to achieve resonance in the subordinates, not strict obedience to a textbook on leadership techniques.

Nevertheless, the above-mentioned evaluation always has a reference point. It is the effect that matters, not the obedience in detail—a lesson that leaders have to learn over and over again. Leadership is open heart surgery on teams and organizations and on the internal images, needs, and expectations of others that appear in them. It is a task that cannot be effectively engineered from affect, but only from a distance, soberly and with a view of the big picture.

Smart leadership is not only governed by internal flexibility and the self-transformation of the leader, but also from the leader's ability to balance two things at once: First, closeness (to employee questions and needs), and secondly, a distance (from the expected expectations that are often entangled in personal relationships).

Table 24.1

The commandments of clever leadership
1. You don't have to be right, but be effective. This is a difficult point because people tend to equate being told that they are wrong with lack of respect, even though the two things—soberly observed—have nothing to do with each other.
2. You can't lose respect that you don't command. This paradoxical statement tells us that our expectation that other people do what we expect of them can only be disappointed if the expectation is actually possible and reasonable.
3. State you expectations precisely in numbers and time periods. Numbers are without passion. That is why many arguments disappear when we talk less and quantify more.
4. Become imperturbable: holding grudges will consume the energy you need to lead. Leaders get paid to operate on the open-hearts of individuals, teams, and organizations. How can you take it personally when someone groans, screams, or fights back?
5. When goals are not reached, react in clear if-then chains. Leadership requires consequences. That is why deviations from targets cannot simply be accepted, but must be clearly identified and associated with consequences.
6. Plan in such a way that you can grant second chances. Commitment is one pillar upon which smart leadership rests; anticipative flexibility is the other. Leadership must anticipate that things can fail despite all efforts. A smart leader distinguishes himself by enabling another attempt.
7. Always have a back-up plan. The best insurance against the failure of your goals and projects is a Plan B. It is your own fault if you have none, because it is not improbable that activities will misfire and deadlines will be missed.
8. Present yourself as versatile and surprise expectations. Expectations dictate actions and tend to smother flexibility and innovation. That is why effective leaders do not focus on expectations, but instead, in some cases, disappoint them.
9. Surround yourself with skeptics, not yes-men. Yes-men confirm your personal preferences, expectations, and impressions. Skeptics issue warnings—usually more often than necessary. But they are the true friends of smart leaders.
10. Don't take the achievement of goals for granted; instead, praise and appreciate. Smart leaders reflect and celebrate triumphs and reward those involved in reaching them. The leader who does not praise and appreciate, is sawing through the leg of the chair on which he is sitting.

Rule 25

Banish the Ice-Cold Manager in You—Become a More Humane Leader

Leaders are confronted daily with requests for advice, which are not always related to mere information, clarification, or decision-making. Leaders are often asked to mediate conflict or to mentor those in difficult phases of life with tact and consideration. This aspect expands the dimensions of leadership several times over and is often overlooked in leadership research and models.

For many employees, leaders are "significant others" (Mead, 1934). In this context, they are not only asked for professional advice, but are also consulted about personal concerns and problems—especially when these troubles make themselves evident in the workplace or become tangential to professional planning.

The head of a large college related the following:

"The head of a faculty of 350 is always in contact with fifteen to twenty people who are suffering from cancer. This is not limited to managing the temporary replacements for colleagues who are merely unable to teach. No, it is the human side that makes it difficult to sleep at night. How do you talk to someone who is telling you how far his cancer has advanced? There is no way to remain simply professional.

These are people you have known for decades in some cases. You know that they still have kids in college or that they have just gone through a divorce—it's often too much for me. And there have been days when I have had to build up and encourage two or three such colleagues. In these conversations, I can forget all the leadership concepts because they come to you as their supervisor, but they want to meet you as a person!"

An effective leader does not avoid such questions, but acknowledges them while keeping in mind that leadership involves supervising the "entire person" (with their concerns, limitations, and fears). The ability to humanize their actions is often a challenge for leaders, and they must recognize that they are responsible not only for achieving organizational goals, but also for the people who are helping them achieve those goals——a constellation that cannot really be "employee focused" solely with textbook rigidity and a technical focus.

Leaders are advocates for their employees and they can never be disappointed. They lead on the basis of a fundamental trust and as a service provider to those who invest a significant part of their time and energy in the common effort, from which they derive their identity and purpose in life.

The demands of such a comprehensive employee orientation impact the fundamental requirements of effective leadership, as the following example shows.

I TAKE CARE OF "MY PEOPLE"

The head of an export company gave this answer during coaching:

"I am, of course, involved in the requirements and goals of the entire company, and would be in real trouble if I were unable to achieve them. Nevertheless, I have learned to engage in the very definition of these things, and in doing so, I always have 'my people' very much in mind. I care for the well-being of my people, which means I consider from the beginning what these requirements will mean for them and how we can achieve those goals with the capabilities my employees have. In doing so, I sometimes have had to challenge my supervisors in order to improve the general conditions under which my employees work. I have also learned that when colleagues experience you fighting for them, you will rarely have any leadership problem.

This view of one's own actions as a leader is constantly overlaid by thoughts and actions that threaten to reduce employees to anonymous figures on a chessboard. To counteract this anonymity, an exercise called "The World of the Employee" was developed as a meditation exercise. It is important because it allows the smart leader to inwardly focus his or her employee orientation (see Table 25.1).

There are still a few individual voices that present the undeniable fundamental contrasts between leaders and followers as insurmountable. They are extremely skeptical of any focus on employees and see such a focus as merely a subtle deception. Ultimately, they say the interests of leaders and those of followers are so different that only the employee representatives could be effectively responsible for employee concerns.

Others label efforts to humanize employees as kitsch and maintain that it is entirely adequate to pursue a "management by information" strategy. This

Table 25.1

Meditation exercise for re-focusing on the employees
1. Appreciation along with instructions *I see the potential and effort of the employees and feel thankful and joy at this good fortune.* *I acknowledge this today by . . .*
2. Limiting the isolated *I also see the efforts and drive of those who make my life difficult, who thwart my plans* *and struggle with my leadership. I will reach out to them today by . . .*
3. Conversations not announcements *I will not succumb to the illusion that everything is going fine just because we are* *accomplishing what we are supposed to accomplish. I realize that the team also requires* *discussion and exchanges with the leadership. Today, I will take care of this requirement* *by . . .*

is adequate, they maintain, if the aim is truly about recognizing employees as mature partners and sparing them from all forms of paternalistic worries, which they always assume to be arrogance.

Such skeptical voices have not won the day in leadership debates, primarily because no one has shown convincingly that the two approaches—employee orientation and information orientation—are mutually exclusive.

Effective leaders pursue an integrative approach and know that employees want to participate and want their efforts to be seen. They want leaders to be aware of their potentials, questions, and real-world concerns. Effective leaders should therefore visibly exercise an employee orientation and a cooperative attitude towards those who, on the basis of laws or collective bargaining agreements, are officially responsible for the concerns of the employees.

Rule 26

Accept the Limits of Leadership and Learn to Manage Dissent

Smart leaders recognize when they are being attacked or challenged, but they do not take it personally. They have the necessary leadership know-how and the skills to deal with resistance effectively and act in the interests of the whole.

Leaders who can manage resistance do not simply act as they have seen others act or as they think they should act. Instead, their behavior is characterized by a competence profile that is essentially composed of the elements in Table 26.1.

Competent and systemic smart leadership is not always successful. Even effective leaders feel helpless and defenseless when confronted with seemingly endless and insurmountable resistance. Their normal interventions, marked by consensus and agreement, have no traction. Often, they consciously avoid exercising the power that is inextricably connected with any claim to leadership.

Of course, desired behavior cannot be forcibly coerced by means of power because the system (organization, teams, and individuals) always does what the structural determinacy allows it to do. The task of leading, however, remains. Smart leaders have the responsibility to supply the aforementioned subsystems with target-actual comparisons (Krusche, 2008, p. 94) and to provide the necessary conditions for minimizing or overcoming the differences.

The condition for success is the ability of the systems to communicate so that responsibilities, power relationships, assignments, and offers of communication by the leadership may be effectively understood. This prerequisite is difficult to assess in the recruiting process because the necessary skills only surface over the course of a career. It can come up in situations in which the

Table 26.1

Smart leadership requires know-how and competence(s)	
Leadership know-how	What does leadership research and theory say about the success factors of leadership actions?
	How is goal-oriented leadership theoretically and practically connected with the concepts of personnel and organizational development, team development and professional development?
	How can projects be successfully and efficiently planned and managed? What concepts and strategies from management theory and socio-psychological research, among other fields, must be mastered?
Systemic abilities	What attitudes of a leader are helpful in the face of the difficulties associated with purposeful interventions in social systems, and how can these attitudes be strengthened?
	How do people construct social reality, and how do personal experiences and beliefs intervene?
	How is it possible to manage the different concepts of reality and interpretive tendencies of the other in a way that would make cooperation, and even developmental change, more likely?
Self-transformation, know-how, and ability	What do brain and emotion researchers and even change management concepts say about the inner workings of one's own thoughts, feelings, and actions?
	What can be done to limit or reduce the distorting effects of one's own beliefs and judgments?
	What discussion and communication techniques can help to avoid escalations, termination of the conversation, and emotionalism?
Resistance management	How do I deal with criticism and doubt (about the matter or the person) in such a way that effectiveness, and not irritants determines my actions?
	How do I involve critically or defensively articulated positions?
	How do I isolate myself from the issue, and separate myself from recognizably non-objective behavior?

leader's plans are sabotaged, instructions not followed, or hierarchical positions undermined and replaced by informal competing hierarchies (putsch groups). Leadership is then charged with limiting these centrifugal tendencies and effectively defining the resulting dissent. Even effective leadership repeatedly finds itself having to clarify the question of affiliation. A leader cannot lead if other units have been established *within* the system for systemic reasons (in self-images and—disappointed—self-constructs, etc.).

Smart leaders take nothing personally, but they can set clear limits if necessary. Leaders have the task of guaranteeing the survival of the whole—not the integration of those who are capable of expressing autonomy, but not the conditions of autonomy in their organizational behavior.[11]

In a leadership workshop, the head of a foreign branch office reported:

"I have to admit that I did not make things easy for my former bosses. In my very first position after graduating from college, I immediately had a tense relationship with the former boss. So I changed jobs, and on leaving—when I did not have to be considerate of him anymore—I came down on him like a ton of bricks in front of all the employees. This took a little longer in my second job. After a few years, however, it was I who disloyally talked behind the boss's back and used every opportunity to undermine his position.

I even dared to perform a trial of strength by winning over colleagues and denouncing my boss to his superiors. Fortunately, that did not work and it was me who had to quit the field. It took a few years before I understood that my 'mean' behavior had to do with me and my inner inability to experience authority than with my boss, who was quite competent and had built me up and supported me. It was not until many years later that I could express my regret about my behavior back then and give up this destructive behavioral pattern completely."

Rule 27

Work with Synergy Markers. Avoid the Trap of Individualizing and Personalizing

Effective leaders, as we have seen, take nothing personally. They are aware that they will have to take care of all sorts of social and personal conflict situations so common in organizations, while taking care to avoid the paralyzing lament that they themselves are victims of adverse conditions. The smart leaders know about the diverse forms of human cooperation—disloyalty and intrigues are as familiar to them as the success that results from the dynamics of teams or individuals.

Effective leaders do not immediately scream out "traitor" when discovering an arbitrary act, but rather try to appreciate the positive energy that comes from such passionate dedication and benefit from the synergy.

An effective leader must practice how to swiftly identify what is really behind self-organization, momentum, and creativity: once manifested in the system negatively, these elements could lead to a polycentricism that will destroy the entire system, or to the dynamic filling of autonomous areas.

During this process, several synergy markers can be identified that facilitate separation of the "wheat from the chaff" in the leader's own interpretations and assessments of actions which may appear to thwart the leader's plans:

Table 27.1

Synergy markers	
Keep a record	Behavior can only be deemed jeopardizing to leadership intentions if it occurs repeatedly. Be observant and compose a list of incidents, but refrain from reacting immediately.
Avoid using "you"	Avoid "you" statements in disputes because they tend to assign guilt, take on the role of victim, and often involve insults, indignation, and overreaction.
Ask again	When your requirements are questioned, first ask what the questions mean, re-clarify your expectations and, if necessary, set limits and identify consequences.
Cut the drama	Misunderstandings, criticism of leaders, and antipathy are perfectly normal in the context of leadership, so refrain from using a sledgehammer to open a nut and avoid dramatization without resolving the dispute.
Toss out rigidity	Avoid rigid responses (small-mindedness, pettiness, etc.) and react flexibly to compulsiveness and obsessions—by clearly defining limits, but also by showing inexhaustible friendliness.
Composure	Observe your emotional levels carefully and avoid important talks and decisions when you feel inner agitation and anger. Arrange for a cool-down.
Look for other interpretations	There is always more than one interpretation. Avoid allies who always support your point of view. It is enough to know that everything could be quite different than you perceive it to be and to act according to this knowledge.
Sense of purpose	If boundaries are overstepped, cooperation refused or even torpedoed, or if commitment to the effort and your leadership role is undermined, enforce the appropriate consequences calmly and decisively. Communicate your intentions to the other party. Dissent must be clearly highlighted and not swept under the carpet.

Rule 28

Learn to Lead Knowing that You Can Be Replaced and Ensure the System You Are Responsible for Will, Temporarily, Live On

Effective leadership is the shaping of development. It cannot be accomplished without both mid- and long-term goals, and corresponding foresight. In the process, however, leaders occasionally forget or ignore the boundaries of their own biography, which is not only about breakthroughs and advances, but also, inevitably, about withdrawals and farewells. The philosopher de Montaigne (1533–1592) wrote:

> Make room for the others as others have made room for you. . . . The utility of life consists not in its length, but in its use; a man may have lived long, and yet lived but little. Make use of time while you have it. It is up to your will, and not upon the number of years you have lived. Did you think you would never arrive at the place towards which you are continually headed? (de Montaigne, 1976, p. 27ff)

In seminars, such texts often cause frowns and irritation. For many leaders, the leap from the immediately pressing issues of everyday life to the deep questions of their own lives and mortality is too great. The following dialog occurred in a seminar for leaders:

> *"I find this topic too gloomy. I am going to live well as long as I can, and when it's over, it's over. Why should I concern myself today with things that hopefully lie many years ahead of me?" asked a young lady who had been in her position of leadership for only two years. "I disagree," replied a colleague from another department who was not much older. "Two years ago, my brother died in a car accident, and since then, I have become more reflective in both my job and my family. I often look at my children, and I enjoy every minute that trickles through*

113

*the hourglass—without panic, but with the clear awareness that I could miss some-
thing if I do not feel exactly how much happiness and energy is expressing itself at
the moment. That is why Montaigne's lines touch me deeply and I have also become
much more affable and sociable—in both family and everyday working life." An
older colleague who had been in semi-retirement for half a year chimed in: "To be
honest, I am really impressed with how consciously you as a young colleague are
dealing with these questions of your own mortality and the fragility of your own life.
It wasn't until I had turned sixty that I gradually began to understand that my
proper role is gradually to withdraw and—on behalf of the common effort for which
we all struggle and from which we all live—to make room for someone else. Since
coming to that realization, I handle the daily demands in a completely different
manner, and I can tell you that it has somehow made me more effective at what
I do."*

Always be aware of your own mortality, and do what is necessary in job and
family—that is what de Montaigne was trying to tell to us. In 1580, he wrote
the following lines: "Becoming aware of death means becoming aware of freedom. A man who has learned about death, shall never be a slave" (ibid, p. 16).

It is also true that "those who have learned about death, understand how
to lead." Deep inside, they have changed their perspective on life. This
change in perspective can be consciously initiated and achieved. Table 28.1
on the following page may be motivating in that effort. Study the entries,
which in effect are the steps to a "mortality-aware" leadership.

Thinking through these aspects of mortality-aware leadership will not
change the inner pictures and drivers all at once; nevertheless, the leader who
does so will become more sensitive to the deeper meaning (or insignificance)
of the experiences of daily life. It is worth keeping these aspects in mind and
think about them every now and then—in phases of reflection and objectivity.

Preparing for the farewells that are surely coming our way can help reduce
our stubbornness, and perhaps even our "bossiness," both personality characteristics that often land us in desperate situations by communicating in a
world in which some share and others reject our views. Such a simplified
understanding of the different camps is what often separates us permanently
from others and results in the dissipation of a substantial portion of the organization's energy and potential.

However, from time to time, we do feel that we are not in contact with the
powerful energy of life. This energy arises in cooperation, not in conflict.
This view of mortality also makes us aware of the mortality of others. What
will remain are not the controversies and conflicts, but what has been created
and allowed to mature through the sensible application of our energy.

Mortality-aware leadership opens our eyes to what actions are actually
worthwhile for getting the synergies to emerge while letting petty conflicts
fade away.

Table 28.1

Characteristics of mortality-aware leadership		− −	−	+	+ +
Fight	Every day I am aware that time is running out, and, as a result, I know what is worth fighting for and how fighting is rewarded.				
Aims	I do not pursue personal success and glory, but see myself in the service of the sustainability of the system for which I am responsible.				
Rectitude	I participate solely in activities that create energy, and avoid escalating conflicts and personal disputes.				
Emotion	I am no stranger to human feelings, and I react to malice and obstacles that stand in my way in a calm manner.				
Willingness to serve	Every day, I consider what support and supervision is necessary for others to contribute to their personal development.				
End of self	I know who I am and what I can do, and I have nothing to prove to myself or others. Narcissistic endeavors are strange to me.				
Labor orientation	I devote myself and all my energy to the problems that need to be solved while concerning myself with the questions and needs of those affected (customers, colleagues, etc.).				
Luck	I know that without the opportunities I have had and without my health and energy, I would not be what I am today. I am extremely thankful for having such good fortune.				

Rule 29

Distrust Rules and Examine Your Own Relationship to Rules

Rules, like so much else, are constructions. They are the congealed and solidified experiences and reflections of those who create and enforce them. Nevertheless, it is possible to distinguish between rules that provide information as a reaction to a specific situation and look fragile and brittle, and other rules, which appear as if they present some universal truth.

The rules of effective leadership do not prescribe, but encourage us to look at the rules—frequently hidden—in our own thoughts and actions. They are rules that provide a better understanding of our own impetus for control and our own set of regulations. They serve to increase the number and type of options available to us despite such limiting factors.[12]

The rules of effective leadership are also reflective in nature: they provide the impulse and the stimulus for reflection—time to consider the situation differently and to react with more reserve and deliberation. These rules avoid the aura of a new leadership doctrine. They rather strengthen a fundamental distrust of any kind of self-enclosed leadership concept and by doing so, leaders can ignore the recommended actions coming at them "from the outside" once and for all.

This disappointment is an enlightening and useful step because it ends the illusion that leadership rules are separate from the individual and hidden outside only to be perceived and applied in order to achieve automatic leadership success. Even leadership research experts can offer no more against this illusion, often deeply ingrained in many people in positions of leadership, than the sobering, but also encouraging, suggestion that no leadership rules can be effective unless the leader has worked them out by means of self-reflection—not by remaining the same person, but by comprehending what the person can become (cf. Arnold, 2010; Hüther, 2011). Smart leadership appreciates the following words from German poet Erich Kästner (1899–1974): "There is no good unless you do it" (Kästner, 1998, p. 277).

These words are often misunderstood as encouraging humane behavior, which makes them appear hollow and trite and they remain ineffective. However, such an interpretation is not faithful to Kästner's philosophy of life, which was simple, undogmatic, and full of self-deprecation—the material that inspires the smart leader. Two Kästner poems "The Farewell" and "Variations on the Farewell," address this theme:

The Farewell

Now that I fully part from you
hear my epilogue:
Dear friends, do not be angry with me
because I have educated myself!

He who endeavors to change,
Fully and completely,
will commit an act of futility,
if he does not become, who he was!

A Variant of the Farewell

A man who has ideals
should be wary about achieving them.
Otherwise, he will one day
No longer resemble himself, but will resemble others. (ibid, p. 279)

It is this disillusionment with rules found outside as well as our own internal rules that we must try to come to terms with and either accept or not accept. A leader who does not come to terms with this and actually spreads more confusion than focus, energy, and perspective has no other choice than to try to discover the rules that are in play and then seek opportunities to create better functioning rules for the job at hand.

This disillusionment is often surprising and irritating, among other things, because it counters the expectation of recipes and reveals a paradoxical meta-rule wholly in the style of Kästner: "A leader cannot *not* regulate, but also cannot regulate. Smart leaders can only observe the rule that says to observe in themselves and others, those rules that lend expression to their own thoughts, feelings, and actions."

In this context, learning to distrust rules while discovering your own rules can be easier if you follow these three steps, which include the rule to avoid rules:

Table 29.1 Rules from the Santiago Principle

Rules to avoid in systemic leadership	
A. Reflection Reflect on mental models	(1) Rules reduce complexity to the detriment of the uniqueness and specificity of situations. Dare to face that specificity. (2) Mental models are blinders (mistakes of egocentricity). (3) Rules are congealed mental models. (4) Look for chances to supervise, coach, and advise.
B. Analysis Reconstruct the systemics	(5) Systematically produce a variety of aspects, sources of energy, and ways of reading situations ("let the system speak"). (6) Always consider the system's potential to solve problems first.
C. Action Plan the system development	(7) Create systematic opportunities for self-control. (8) Create transparency and always strive for (broad) consensus, but clearly identify disagreement. (9) Consciously develop levels of relationship and acceptance.

Afterword

Leaders are people too.[13]

The emotional depths of life are constantly affected as we learn to perform, to assert ourselves as leaders, or to experience authority and restrictions. At such times, we perceive something of the "stuff" from which self-confidence develops. The "right stuff" is the experiences of self-efficacy in the confrontation with another, perhaps a strong parental figure. This experience is just as important for development as a nurturing parental figure. When others differentiate themselves from us, evaluate or give us feedback, set limits for us or confront us with expectations, we, in return, experience ourselves as being distinct and we learn to differentiate and define ourselves. The emotional and stirring moments always remind us or make us relive such *differentiating experiences.*

The case of Michael Kohlhaas, as described in a novella by Heinrich von Kleist, is well-known. He is betrayed and thereafter fights doggedly for his rights, sparing no escalation, and ultimately losing his life. To be sure, Michael Kohlhaas does suffer injustice, but his rigid and relentless response knows no limits. It breaks new ground for a pattern of inner rigidity that no longer has anything to do with the injustice. But there are others like him, who with the same vehemence seek to rectify their own perceived injustices—a familiar scenario in organizations and companies.

These crises of self-worth can become organizational crises if, for example, a promising, overconfident employee decides he would rather take the organization down than truly confront the personal crisis that finds expression in his behavior. The world that apparently refuses what you expect—often personified by the leadership—is to blame and he takes the battle to them with intrigues and campaigns (see Kets de Vries, 2004).

THE EARLY IMPRINTING OF INNER IMAGES
OF LEADERSHIP

In these and other less extreme conflicts, the fundamental characteristics of our personalities find expression, characteristics that we also have in leadership and teaching situations. We acquired these fundamental emotional behavior patterns early in life. We may have a fear of failure because overwhelming expectations were placed on us and we failed to master them—and didn't have any supporting or consoling factors for our failure. On the other hand, perhaps we are essentially confident and approachable because we grew up in an atmosphere that gave us the fundamental feeling that, no matter what we do or how successful we actually are in our endeavors, nothing will happen to us because we are loved, appreciated, and protected (see Roth, 2007, p. 24f).

Smart leaders can see beyond façades—their own as well as those of others. They can approach others in an appreciative manner (see Deissler and Gergen, 2004) if they understand the emotional searching situation of the moment. The human side of the "doting" student, the "chaotic" employee, or the "scheming" colleague will be apparent. It is easier to lay aside the judgmental glasses so often worn automatically when observing behavior that disturbs or irritates us. At the same time, leaders can use their ability to see beyond façades to trace their own emotional background. They can recognize the experiences that shape their reactions when they remain aloof, attach too much importance to certain formalities (titles, protocol), or are too easily disappointed and basically flee from others.

When leaders are able to access such mechanisms, a new and more professional basis for understanding and dealing with colleagues, employees, trainees, and partners can emerge. Perhaps a leader can even recognize some common ground with the "difficult" other—for essentially, people all function on the same or similar principles. They want to stay the way they are and they continuously grant themselves the "paralyzing permission" to do so (Arnold, 2009b, p. 10).

Every person expresses his or her fundamental emotional attitude towards the world through body language—this is true of unambiguous emotional conditions as well as of moods and temperaments. It is a typical attitude, a walk, gesture, and expression that communicates the extent of a person's current emotional state. This is because a person's initial form of emotional expression is non-verbal or the "aura" or "vibes," as some psychologists call them. Our auras give expression to the emotional energies that form our possible realities and our self-presentation. The givens can only affect us to the extent we have learned to accept them (see Arnold, 2005).

Leaders cannot grasp their own basic attitude towards the world until they "listen" to their own non-verbal presentation. Ask a colleague to describe the impression he or she gets from your typical body language and facial expressions.

While modern brain research has confirmed the importance of childhood experiences for adult behavior (see also Kaplan-Solms and Solms, 2003), not every leader or employee presents such obvious dependency or controlling behavior in conflict situations that it raises the suspicion that these behaviors are the continuation of insecure or ambivalent separation experiences. It is not the responsibility of the leaders or trainers to uncover such deep dimensions of observed behavior—this requires complex therapeutic sessions. It is nevertheless helpful to know about such contexts and influences, because they allow us to view the "difficult employee" (Lelord and André, 2008) with more kindness. Perhaps we will even succeed in seeing the hand of fate in the "unbelievable behavior" of others such as disloyalty, arrogance, aggressive, or overly sensitive reactions, and then wisely approach them with some understanding.

Every behavior is the expression of some effort to maintain an internal balance between the self and its emotional fate—even when repeating the past and putting a strain on the situation—often without recognizing this mechanism and without really being able to change behavior.

This comprehension, which enables us to perceive and approach ourselves and others in a new way, has been termed "emotional competence" in professional training and personnel development circles since the mid-1990s. Daniel Goleman, in his best-seller *Emotional Intelligence*, refers to the "obsolete neural alarms" (Goleman, 1998, p. 40) programmed into the brain's amygdala that constantly interfere with our behavior and lead us to "imprecise" reactions:

> If the current situation is similar to a past situation in even one important element, it [the amygdala] reports a match—which is why this switch setting is imprecise. It eagerly gives the order to react to the present in a manner which was learned long ago, including the thoughts, emotions, and reactions that have been learned as the response to an event that may have little resemblance to the current one, but are similar enough to alarm the amygdala. (ibid, p. 41)

Emotional intelligence is the knowledge of the power of emotions and of the mechanisms by which they function. Emotional competence is the ability to recognize one's own tendency towards imprecise responses and to avoid such reactions in the current situation or to correct them when they do occur. The prerequisite for emotional competence is emotional intelligence.

Among the talents that indicate emotional intelligence, according to Daniel Goleman, are self-control, enthusiasm, tenacity, and self-motivation" (ibid, p. 12). He is even more explicit in other points, for example, when he cites the earlier efforts of Peter Salovey, a psychologist from Yale and the true creator of the concept of emotional intelligence, to define the concept more precisely (Salovey and Mayer, 1990). Salovey distinguished five categories of emotional competence and their characteristic elements in Table A.1.

GETTING TO EMOTIONAL RESONANCE

Emotions, as we have discussed, can be sensed—physically—and, in some subtle way, cloud or deceive human perception. For example, someone afraid of riding in the sidecar of a motorcycle will have a different sense of well-being than the daredevil. Something similar happens with the other emotions of grief, joy, or irritation, to name only a few. They all concern the same issue: the state of mind or mood of the individual colors their perception of a particular situation with a certain energy.

What fascinates one plunges the other into panic; what most people consider merely uncomfortable may seem intolerable to others. The psychoanalyst Fritz Riemann characterizes such internal movements as "overvaluations" and describes how we all overvalue one or the other of our sensibilities: He proposes that it is precisely this that characterizes us as unique (Riemann, 1998). However, people sometimes overvalue in difficult leadership situations and maneuver themselves into difficult places, painful to them and their families.

How can those responsible help avoid such self-destructive behavior in learning or leadership processes? Daniel Goleman studied such forms of emotional leadership in his other books (Goleman et al., 1998). In one of them, *Emotional Leadership*, he coins the term "resonant leadership" and writes, "When leaders fail to exercise the necessary empathy or are unable to decode the emotions of the group, they produce dissonance and transmit messages that upset the receiver unnecessarily" (Goleman, Boyatzis, and McKee, 2002, p. 39).

He illustrates this with the example of a remarkably resonant leader:

He adjusted to people's feelings and steered them in a positive direction. What he said was based on his own values so that he came across as genuine and convincing. He generated resonance with his listeners so that they could receive his messages positively and feel confident and inspired—even at such a difficult moment as this. When a leader calls forth resonance, it can be read on people's faces: they are attentive and interested and their eyes are bright and shining. . . .

Table A.1   Peter Salovey's Five Areas of "Emotional Intelligence"

The Five Categories of "Emotional Intelligence"	Characterization
Recognizing one's own emotions	"Self-recognition—the ability to recognize your own feelings as they are occurring—is the foundation of emotional intelligence." The ability "to constantly monitor one's own feelings is decisive for psychological insight and the understanding of the self. Those who cannot recognize their own feelings must surrender to them. Those who are sure of their feelings have an easier time approaching their lives and understand more clearly what they truly think about individual decisions, from the choice of spouse to the choice of career."
Managing emotions	"Managing feelings so that they are appropriate to the situation is an ability based on self-perception." It is the ability "to calm down, to shake off the fear, melancholy, or irritation that creeps up (. . .). Those who are weak in this respect constantly struggle with oppressive feelings; the stronger ones recover much more quickly from the setbacks and excitement of life."
Converting emotion to action	"Placing emotions in the service of a goal is . . . essential for our interest, self-motivation, skills, and creativity. Emotional self-control—delaying gratification and suppressing impulsiveness – is the foundation of every kind of success. If you put yourself in the flow, you become capable of outstanding achievement. Whatever the challenge, it is approached more productively and effectively."
Empathy	"Knowing what others are feeling—another talent that springs from emotional self-awareness—is the foundation for knowing human nature." This ability has to do with the "roots of empathy," or the social costs of the inability to distinguish among various emotions and the reasons why empathy calls forth altruism. Empathic leaders tend to pick up on the latent social signals that show what others need or wish. Those who fit in this category are more successful in care-giving professions or as a salesman or manager."
Dealing with relationships	"The art of relationships consists largely of the ability to deal with the emotions of others." This area asks the questions of "social competence and incompetence and (the) specific abilities . . . involved. They are the foundation of popularity, leadership, and interpersonal effectiveness. Those who are highly skilled in this area are successful in everything that requires smooth cooperation with others—they are the 'social' stars."

(from Goleman 1998, p. 65f)

Resonant leadership is recognized, among other things, by the group's resonating the leader's optimism and positive energy. One maxim of emotionally intelligent leadership is that resonance strengthens and extends the emotional impact of leadership. The stronger the resonance, the better the connection is between people. Resonance minimizes noise in the system. A team means "more signal, less noise."

The glue that holds the people on a team together and produces loyalty to one another and the organization is their emotions. . . . There arises an emotional bond that helps them to remain focused even in times of fundamental change and uncertainty. Work becomes more meaningful and satisfying. . . . An emotionally intelligent leader is distinguished by an ability to create this bond within the group. (ibid, p. 39ff)

This discussion shows that emotional leadership can also bring about allegiance. In a training situation or through cooperation in the workplace, people experience a form of interaction that is new to them and continues to be new and unusual. While experiencing such allegiance cannot overcome the emotional independence of some individuals, it does provide a framework to them that does not repeat or solidify their original emotional experiences. In such a culture, those who are insecure or ambivalent can gradually learn to experience themselves differently in relation to others and to the demands they encounter. These people tend to see in the leadership what they always knew deep down—and their fixed focus will repeatedly confirm it for them. However, they will also gradually but inevitably come to realize that their actual leader trusts them to complete tasks and does not see mistakes as occasions for punishment, but as chances to learn and develop. They gradually learn that even their supervisors have a true interest in them and their development and will never abandon them.

EMOTIONAL LITERACY FOR LEADERS

A *leadership culture of remedial experienced relationships* requires leaders who command emotional competence. They must be familiar with the inner reactions that compete to influence them if they are to avoid certain reactions. A leader must learn, for example, not to react to the provocations of a disrespectful employee with mere indignation and punishment, since that will only reinforce what the person already knows and wishes to provoke with his or her impudence. Emotional discipline is necessary to avoid a reaction based on inner logic.

Rather, the smart leader bases the reaction on an understanding of the emotional search being expressed by the other person. Provocations are often the soul's call for help; a call to see a familiar situation: "I may feel bad, but at least I know the feeling." Leaders who oblige such provocations in their daily leadership function are giving "permission" to the offender to remain unchanged and to avoid further development in his or her thoughts, feelings, and actions.

Resonant leadership distances itself from the more common style that focuses primarily on managing the weaknesses and deficits of others. In contrast, resonant leadership is oriented on potential and follows the insights of so-called positive psychology (Seligmann, 2003): Positive psychology in companies concerns itself with consciously creating the conditions for people to be able to develop their talents, to feel appreciated, and to learn to grow beyond themselves.

To this purpose, Utho Creusen and Nina-Ric Eschemann have formulated several guiding questions that help employees to assess their potential with a view to developing their strengths (Creusen and Eschemann, 2010, p. 24):

- What activities did I look forward to today?
- What did I really enjoy doing, and what gave me energy?
- Was there an activity after which I felt wonderful?
- What opportunities will arise tomorrow to do things that I especially like to do and am good at?
- Who do I know that does what I like to do even better than I can, and what can I learn from that person?

Daily reflection based on such guiding questions gradually allows the individual to develop a kind of routine in which he or she more consciously adapts to energy-generating activities. It leads to the enjoyment of work-flow experiences and what Martin Seligman describes as "resilience," which is fundamental to the development of individual self-confidence and potential (see Frick, 2007).

Investigate the following questions with your team: What measures would allow the training culture of a company to change so that people could develop their talents, feel appreciated, and learn to grow beyond themselves? What does goal orientation mean to you in your role as a leader?

Emotional leadership is conditional upon a number of abilities whose development can be stimulated by several activities—performed independently as well as in training. These abilities help leaders to become more self-reflective and more effective in their leadership (see Table A.2).

Self-reflection training is concerned with taking a detached view of one's own thoughts, feelings, and actions. It allows the individual to view things in a less passionate way because it creates a certain distance and has no need for justification. The self-reflective view takes ownership of one's own reactions; usually, this is recognized only after the reaction has taken place and then

Table A.2   The Ten Commandments of Emotional Leadership

Emotional alphabetization	
Information	(1) Inform yourself about the variety of emotions that exist, what material the emotion consists of, and how emotions affect people's behavior.
Escape	(2) Become familiar with the five ways of escaping emotional traps (such as "postponing answers") and practice them in your daily interactions.
Advice for learning	(3) Avoid parent-like or even offensive behavior, and strengthen feelings of self-effectiveness in those you lead.
Emotional Self-Reflection	
Self-analysis	(4) Identify the typical basic patterns of your spirit. Develop a map of your preferred ego states for your inner portfolio.
Release	(5) Decide not to be available to your preferred ego states and train alternatives.
Growth	(6) Make the decision to enter into the variety of your habits (in the form of an "inner excursion", for example).
Emotional Resonance Ability	
Attentiveness	(7) Be considerate of the distinct emotional competences of the other person and avoid judgmental reactions.
Fear reduction	(8) Reduce fear—particularly in fear-laden situations (such as tests).
Relational work	(9) Strive to strengthen and foster connections and relationships in your team (team/departmental training, working groups) by means of conscious measures.
Integration	(10) Avoid ostracism. Leave no one behind; deal specifically with those who attract attention through provocation, and consciously promote talent.

only after a certain amount of practice prior to the impulsive action. A leader who has practiced self-reflection notices, for example, when his inner monologue is concerned only with a single issue, or when inner chains of argument or visions of making a "blow for freedom" return to coalesce into an ever more urgent impetus to action. Such emotionally charged tensions can result in flat declarations being made to bosses and friends, and partners being surprised by confrontational explanations.

Emotional self-reflectiveness characterizes the ability to recognize and gradually avoid one's own emotional tendencies. The smart leader is aware of the power of emotions and their favored position to interfere and does not feel compelled to quarrel about reality, but uses the surging emotions to be free of them. Smart leaders have the talent to think, feel, and act outside the box of their own emotional beliefs.

Self-reflection can be a release when the leader, in the context of self-analysis, is able not only to document his or her own typical interpretational and emotional patterns, but also to gradually relinquish it and train him- or herself in alternative reactions. Emotional leadership thrives on having empathy for those we lead.

Emotional leadership is based on this ability to sense the emotional situation of the other person and to avoid the limiting—negative—emotionalism. Those who understand emotional leadership are capable of forming a relationship with those they lead, personally creating loyalties and facilitating integration in actors who hardly know what these things are because, in the course of their lives, they may have learned to experience themselves as uncommitted and only weakly integrated, if at all.

Emotional leadership is the ability to lead from the emotional world of those being led. A fundamental prerequisite for this ability is to have sensed and recognized as many facets as possible of the emotional situation of others, and this ability can only be developed by those who have discovered the colorations of the emotions in their own inner world.

Notes

1. Translator's note: Care has been taken, however, to create English approximates of the original German acronyms.

2. This self-inclusion thesis comes from the neuroscientist and constructivist Francisco Varela (1946–2002), who used it to point out the unavoidable linkage between what appears to us to be true in our this-and-not-otherwise biologically and biographically constructed experience—an idea that, with its neurophysiological empiricism added strong, new evidence for the familiar thesis of self-generated reality (see, among others, Varela, 1992).

3. The transformative theory of leadership assumes ". . . that all members of the organization are there voluntarily and, of their own accord, make a contribution to the attainment of a future condition that is seen as worth striving for. On the basis of this assumption that all members are following the same vision and want to give their best for the attainment of this long-term target condition, detailed requirements, continuous monitoring, and additional external incentives are dispensed with. Organizations with a strongly developed transformative culture view the world as complex, volatile, and unpredictable. From this arises the fundamental and humble admission of the uncontrollability of the future, which in turn brings with it a distinct skepticism towards planning requirements, systems of planning aims, and leadership authority figures who decide everything" (Heidbrink and Jenewein, 2011, p. 17).

4. See www.systemischestrukturaufstellungen.com/problemaufstellung.html.

5. Maxims are statements that the person setting up the constellation puts into the mouths of those representing the individual positions by means of which those representatives get, in addition to a spatial sense, a content-based orientation on how one feels in the situation they are depicting—their representative position.

6. "Transformative learning" is defined as learning that induces more far-reaching change in the learner than other kinds of learning, especially learning experiences which shape the learner and produce a significant impact or paradigm shift which affects the learner's subsequent experiences" (www.lifecircles-inc.com/Learningtheories/humanist/mezirow.html).

7. See www.uni-koeln.de/hf/konstrukt/didaktik/systemaufstellung/begruendung.html.

8. So-called hypothesizing is a creative form of complementing possible constructions of reality, with the help of which ossified attitudes and perspectives can be softened and useful alternatives can mature. Ulrich Pfeiffer-Schaupp, head of the Freiburg Institute for Systemic Therapy and Counseling, writes, "By means of conscious hypothesizing, one's own predispositions are made explicit and complemented with new and different assumptions . . . Hypotheses are formed (a) in the context of referral: What does the referrer want? (b) according to task: therapeutic, monitoring, pedagogical? What are the explicit, implicit, and covert tasks? (c) patterns in the client system or problem system; (d) possible solutions" (Pfeifer-Schaupp, 2012, p. 163).

9. The term "self-contained reflection" was employed variously by Francisco Varela in the cognition debate and taken up in adult pedagogy (see Siebert, 2011). Varela et al. record in their book *Der mittlere Weg der Erkenntnis,*

> We suggest changing the kind of reflection and not understanding it merely as abstract activities, but as personified (attentive), open processes. By *personified*, we mean reflection in which body and spirit converge. Reflection does not merely occur through experience, but is itself a form of experience—and this reflective form of experience can be won with attentiveness and awareness. Carried out in this way, it breaks through the chain of familiar thought patterns and prejudices and becomes open reflection, open to other possibilities than those contained in familiar representations of living space. We call this form *attentive, open reflection.* (Varela et al., 1992, p. 49)

In view of the prevailing research practice, Valera et al. observe, "But in the course of research activity, we often forget who is asking the question and how it is being asked. Because we do not want to involve ourselves in the reflection, it remains partial, and our questions become abstract. . . . Ironically, this search for an abstract view from nowhere leads to a view from a very specific, theoretically limited somewhere that is influenced by prejudice" (ibid, p. 49f).

10. Machiavelli is an interventionist who unknowingly coins phrases for a pre-democratic theory of politics; that is, he sums up and accentuates the rules of the successful exercise of power. His historical background is absolutism—a fact that significantly relativizes his discourse. Nevertheless, Machiavelli also describes the most diverse scenarios in which power is exercised and analyzes with an inexorable objectivity the risks and unintended consequences of leadership, however well-intentioned or decisively executed it might be.

11. Systemic organization advisor Berhard Krusche speaks of "conditioned autonomy" in this context and marks the paradoxical requirement this leadership involves with the words: "Facing the lapse of possibilities to remind employees of their duties in a hierarchical way ('Do this! Do that!'), the question arises: how can leadership focus on the attention of individual sectors without permanently distracting their orientation from the whole. Instead of provoking autonomy about simple attitudes, leadership must condition the necessary autonomy in such a way that it backs the whole with its own logic" (Krusche, 2008, p. 117).

12. This approach takes up that of the imperative of Heiz von Foerster.

13. This final chapter is a revision and further development of work presented as Arnold, 2010a.

Bibliography

Argyris, C., and Schön, D. *Die Lernende Organisation*. 2nd ed. Munich: 2002.

Arnold, R. Transformative Erwachsenenbildung. In: R. Arnold; S. Nolda; E. Nuissl (editors) *Wörterbuch Erwachsenenbildung*. Bad Heilbrunn: OBB, 2001, 314–315.

Arnold, R. *Die emotionale Konstruktion der Wirklichkeit*. Baltmannsweiler: 2005.

Arnold, R. Personalentwicklung – neu gedacht. *Pädagogische Materialien der TU Kaiserslautern*, number 28. Kaiserslautern: 2006.

Arnold, R. *Führen mit Gefühl. Eine Anleitung zum Selbstcoaching. Mit einem Methoden-ABC*. Wiesbaden: 2008.

Arnold, R. *Das Santiagoprinzip. Systemische Führung im Lernenden Unternehmen*. 2nd ed. Baltmannsweiler: 2009a.

Arnold, R. *"Seit wann haben Sie das?" Grundlinien eines Emotionalen Konstruktivismus*. Heidelberg: 2009b.

Arnold, R. Emotionale Führung. *Journal für Schulentwicklung*, 14 (2010a), 2, 31–39.

Arnold, R. *Selbstbildung. Oder: Wer kann ich werden und wenn ja wie?* Baltmannsweiler: 2010b.

Arnold, R. Zehn Regeln für eine elegante Gesprächskultur. *Personalführung*, 43 (2010c), 11b, 20–29.

Arnold, R. Veränderung durch angewandte Erkenntnistheorie. In: R. Arnold (ed.). *Veränderung durch Selbstveränderung. Impulse für das Changemanagement*. Baltmannsweiler: Schneider, 2011, 1–7.

Arnold, R. *Wie man führt, ohne zu dominieren. 29 Regeln für ein kluges Leadership*. Heidelberg: 2012.

Arnold, R., and Arnold-Haecky, B. *Der Eid des Sisyphos*. Baltmannsweiler: 2009.

Badura, A. *Self-Efficacy. The Exercise of Control*. New York: 1997.

Baecker, D. *Postheroisches Management. Ein Vademecum*. Berlin: 1994.

Bartley, W.W. *Wittgenstein – ein Leben*. Munich: 1999.

Bass, B., and Avolio, B. *Improving Organizational Effectiveness through Transformative Leadership*. Thousand Oaks: 1994.

Bell, A. *Great Leadership. What It Is and What It Takes in a Complex World*. Boston/London: 2006.

Blumenberg, H. *Theorie der Lebenswelt*. Berlin: 2010.

Bördlein, C. *Das sockenfressende Monster in der Waschmaschine: Eine Einführung ins skeptische Denken.* Aschaffenburg: Alibri-Verlag, 2002.

Buber, M. *Das dialogische Prinzip.* Gütersloh: 2002.

Burkert, M. *Qualität von Kennzahlen. Nutzung und Erfolg von Managern.* Wiesbaden: 2008.

Castells, M. *Das Informationszeitalter. Vol. 1: Der Aufstieg der Netzwerkgesellschaft.* Weinheim/Basel: 2004.

Cologne Institute for Economic Research, 2001 www.iwkoeln.de/de/infodienste/iwd/archiv/beitrag/27970.

Coyle, D. *Die Talent-Lüge.* Bergisch-Gladbach: 2009.

Cranton, P. *Understanding and Promoting Transformative Learning. A Guide for Educators of Adults.* New York: 1994.

Creusen, U., and Eschemann, N.-R. Positive Leadership in der Unternehmenspraxis: Talente erkennen und zu stärken ausbauen. *Personalführung,* 1 (2010), 21–25.

Creusen, U., and Eschemann, N.-R. *Zum Glück gibt's Erfolg. Wie Positive Leadership zu Höchstleistungen führt.* Zurich: 2008.

Csikszentmihalyi, M. *Kreativität.* Stuttgart: 1999.

de Montaigne, M. *Essais.* Frankfurt: 1976.

Deissler, K.G., and Gergen, K.J. (ed.). *Die wertschätzende Organisation.* Bielefeld: 2004.

Doppler, K. Über Helden und Weise. Von heldenhafter Führung *im* System zu weiser Führung *am* System. *Organisationsentwicklung,* 2 (2009), 4–13,

Eade, D. *Oxfam Development Guidelines: Capacity Building. An Approach to People Centred Development.* Oxford: 1997.

Eckstein, R. "Wozu brauchen wir Kennzahlen?" Die Relevanz von Kennzahlen im System Schule. *Schulmanagement. Die Zeitschrift für Schulleitung und Schulpraxis,* 2 (2010), 27–32.

Frick, J. *Die Kraft der Ermutigung. Grundlagen und Beispiele zur Hilfe und Selbsthilfe.* Bern: 2007.

Gaugler, E., Oechsler, W., and Weber, W. (ed.). *Handwörterbuch des Personalwesens.* Stuttgart: 2004.

Goleman, D. *Emotionale Intelligenz.* Munich: 1998.

Goleman, D., *Working with Emotional Intelligence.* New York: 1998.

Goleman, D., Boyatzis, R., and McKee, A. *Emotionale Führung.* Munich: 2002.

Gracians, B. *Die Kunst der Weltklugheit in dreihundert Lebensregeln.* Wien: n.d.

Gutschelhofer, A. Mitarbeitergespräch. In: Gaugler, Oechsler, and Weber (eds.): Hand— Wörterbuch des Personal—Wesens. 2004, 1221–1231.

Hamel, G. *Das Ende des Managements. Unternehmensführung im 21. Jahrhundert.* Berlin: 2008.

Happich, G. *Ärmel hoch! Die 20 schwierigsten Führungsthemen und wie Top-Führungskräfte sie anpacken.* Zurich: 2011.

Heidbrink, M.; Jenewein, W. High-performance-Organisationen. Wie Unternehmen eine Hochleistungskultur aufbauen. Stuttgart, 2011.

Horelli, L. Network Evaluation from the Everyday-Life Perspective. A Tool for Capacity Building and Voice. Unpublished manuscript. 2003.

Hüther, G. *Die Macht der inneren Bilder. Wie Visionen das Gehirn, den Menschen und die Welt verändern.* Göttingen: 2006.

Hüther, G. Belohnung ist genauso falsch wie Bestrafung. Ein Interview. *Managerseminare*, 159 (June 2011), 44–46.

Hüther, G. *Was wir sind und was wir sein könnten. Ein neurobiologischer Mutmacher.* Frankfurt: 2011.

Institut der Deutschen Wirtschaft..Die Neuen sind willkommen. *iwd-dienst*, 18 (5 May 2011a), 4–5.

Institut der Deutschen Wirtschaft. Finden, fördern, festhalten. *iwd-dienst*, 8 (24 February 2011b), 8.

Joka, H.J. (ed.). *Führungskräftehandbuch.* Berlin: 2002.

Jumpertz, S. Mit Zweifeln zum Ziel. Misstrauen als Methode. *Managermagazin*, 159 (June 2011), 50–56.

Kaplan, R.S., and Norton, D.P. *Die strategiefokussierte Organisation. Führen mit der Balanced Scorecard.* Stuttgart: 2001.

Kaplan-Solms, K., and Solms, M. *Neuro-Psychoanalyse. Eine Einführung mit Fallstudien.* Stuttgart: 2003.

Kästner, E. Moral. In: Kästner E. (ed. *Zeitgenossen haufenweise. Gedichte. Werke*, Vol. 11. Munich: Carl Hanser, 1998), 277.

Keicher, I. Eine neue Arbeitskultur schaffen. *Weiterbildung. Zeitschrift für Grundlagen, Praxis und Trends*, 2 (2011), 6–8.

Kets de Vries, M. *Führer, Narren und Hochstapler. Die Psychologie der Führung.* Stuttgart: 2004.

Kets de Vries, M. *The Leader on the Couch. A Clinical Approach to Changing People and Organizations.* San Francisco: 2006.

Kets de Vries, M. *The Leader on the Couch. A Clinical Approach to Changing People and Organizations.* San Francisco: 2008.

Kossak, P. Bildungsberatung revisited. Ein Strukturmodell zur Bildungsberatung. In: Arnold, R., Gieseke, W., and Zeuner, C. (ed.). *Bildungsberatung im Dialog. Vol. 1: Theorie – Empirie – Reflexion.* Baltmannsweiler: 2009, 45–67.

Krusche, B. *Paradoxien der Führung. Aufgaben und Funktionen für ein zukünftiges Management.* Heidelberg: 2008.

Lang, K. *Personalführung. Nicht nur reden, sondern leben! Methoden für eine erfolgreiche Kompetenz- und Potenzialentwicklung – mit praxiserprobten Instrumenten und Umsetzungsbeispielen.* 2nd ed. Vienna: 2004.

Lelord, F., and André, C. *Der ganz normale Wahnsinn. Vom Umgang mit schwierigen Menschen.* 5th ed. Berlin: 2008.

Löhr, J. Das Ende der Powerpoint-Parade. *Frankfurter Allgemeine*, (17 December 2010), 20.

Luhmann, N. *Die Gesellschaft der Gesellschaft.* Vol. 2. Frankfurt: 1998.

Luhmann, N., and Schorr, K.E. Das Technologiedefizit der Erziehung und der Pädagogik. *Zeitschrift für Pädagogik*, 25 (1979), 3, 345–365.

Machiavelli, N. *Der Fürst* (1514). Frankfurt: 1990.

Mahlmann, R. *Führungsstile gezielt einsetzen. Mitarbeiterorientiert, situativ und authentisch führen.* Weinheim: Beltz-Verlag, 2011.

Main, M., and Solomon, J. Discovery of a New, Insecure-Disorganized/Disoriented Attachment Pattern. In: Brazelton, T.B., and Yogman, M. (ed.). *Affective Development in Infancy.* Norwood: 1986, 95–124.

Malik, F. *Führen – Leisten – Leben.* 11th ed. Frankfurt: 2001.

Mead, G. H. (1936): *Mind, Self and Society.* University of Chicago Press.

Molcho, S. *Körpersprache im Beruf.* Munich: 2001.

Neal, C., and Neal, P. *The Art of Convening. Authentic Engagement in Meetings, Gatherings and Conversations.* San Francisco: 2011.

Neubarth, A. *Führungskompetenz aufbauen. Wie Sie Ressourcen klug nutzen und Ziele stimmig erreichen.* Wiesbaden: Gabler-Verlag, 2011.

Nowotny, H. *Es ist so. Es könnte auch anders sein.* Frankfurt: 1999.

Ohly, S. Gutes Klima für neue Ideen. Eigeninitiative und Kreativität bei der Arbeit. *Weiterbildung. Zeitschrift für Grundlagen, Praxis und Trends,* 2 (2011), 14–17.

Owen, H. *The Spirit of Leadership. Führen heißt Freiräume schaffen.* 22nd ed. Heidelberg: 2008.

Pelz, W. Transformationale Führung. *Eine Weiterentwicklung des Führens mit Zielvereinbarungen. Zusammenfassende Ergebnisse einer empirischen Studie mit 4.107 Teilnehmern.* www.management-innovation.com/download/Transformationale-Fuehrung .pdf.

Pfeiffer-Schaupp, U. Hypothetisieren. In: Wirth and Kleve, 2012, 161–164.

Piaget, J. *L' équilibration des structures cognitives. Problème central du développement.* Paris: 1975.

Pörksen, B. *Schlüsselwerke des Konstruktivismus.* Wiesbaden: 2011.

Precht, R.D. *Wer bin ich und wenn ja wie viele?* Munich: 2007.

Probst, G. *Selbst-Organisation. Ordnungsprozesse in sozialen Systemen aus ganzheitlicher Sicht.* Berlin: 1987.

Radatz, S. *Wie Organisationen das Lernen lernen. Entwurf eines epistemologischen Theoriemodells organisationalen Lernens aus relationaler Sicht.* Baltmannsweiler: 2011.

Riemann, F. *Grundformen der Angst. Eine tiefenpsychologische Studie.* Munich: 1998.

Rohrschneider, U., and Lorenz, M. *Der Personalentwickler. Instrumente, Methoden, Strategien.* Wiesbaden: 2011.

Roth, G. *Persönlichkeit, Entscheidung und Verhalten. Warum es so schwierig ist, sich und andere zu ändern.* Stuttgart: 2007.

Roth, G. *Bildung braucht Persönlichkeit. Wie lernen gelingt.* Stuttgart: 2011.

Roth, G., and Lück, M. Mit Gefühl und Motivation lernen. Neurobiologische Grundlagen der Wissensvermittlung im Training. *Weiterbildung. Zeitschrift für Grundlagen, Praxis und Trends,* 1 (2010), 40–43.

Salovey, P., and Mayer, J. Emotional Intelligence. *Imagination, Cognition and Personality,* 9 (1990), 185–211.

Sartre, J.P. *Questions de méthode. Cillection idées.* Paris: Édition Gallimard, 1960.

Scharmer, C.O. *Theory U. Leading from the Future as It Emerges. The Social Technology of Presencing.* San Francisco: 2007.

Scharmer, C.O., and Käufer, K. Lernen als Begegnung mit dem Werdenden Selbst. In: Arnold, R. (ed.). *Veränderung durch Selbstveränderung. Impulse für das Changemanagement.* Baltmannsweiler: 2011, 35–49.

Schmidt, S.J. Kreativität aus der Beobachterperspektive. In: Gumbrecht, H.-U. (ed.). *Kreativität – ein verbrauchter Begriff?* Munich: 1988, 33–52.

Schulz von Thun, F. *Miteinander Reden 1: Störungen und Klärungen.* Reinbek: 1990.

Seligman, M. *Der Glücksfaktor: Warum Optimisten länger leben*. Bergisch Gladbach: 2003.

Senge, P. *Die fünfte Disziplin. Kunst und Praxis der lernenden Organisation*. 2nd ed. Stuttgart: 1996.

Senge, P., Kleiner, A., Roberts, C., Ross, R., and Smith, B. *A Fifth Discipline Resource: The Dance of Change*. London: 1999.

Senge, P., Scharmer, O., Jaworski, J., and Sue Flowers, B. *Presence. Exploring Profound Change in People, Organizations and Society*. London: 2005.

Senge, P., Smith, B., Kruschwitz, N., Laur, J., and Schley, S. *The Necessary Revolution. How Individuals and Organisations Are Working Together to Create a Sustainable World*. New York: 2008.

Sennett, R. Schlauer als der Chef erlaubt. Die mächtigen sind selten die Klügsten: Trotz moderner Kommunikationsmittel wird wertvolles Wissen häufig vergeudet. *Die Zeit*, 13 (24 March 2011), 56.

Siebert, H. Selbsteinschließende Reflexion als pädagogische Kompetenz. In: Arnold, R. (ed.). *Veränderung durch Selbstveränderung. Impulse für das Changemanagement*. Baltmannsweiler: 2011, 9–18.

Siefer, W. *Das Genie in mir. Warum Talent erlernbar ist*. Frankfurt: 2009.

Simon, F.B. *Die Kunst, nicht zu lernen und andere Paradoxien in Psychotherapie, Management, Politik*. 3rd ed. Heidelberg: 2002.

Simon, W. *GABALs großer Methodenkoffer. Grundlagen der Kommunikation*. Offenbach: 2004.

Staehle, W. *Management*. Munich: 1989.

Stehli, M. *Das Reflektierende Team und seine Wirkfaktoren: Theorie und Praxis eines systemisch-lösungsorientierten Instrumentariums*. Bern: 2008.

Stringer, P.M. Capacity Building for School Improvement: A Case Study of a New Zealand Primary School. Paper presented to the Asia-Pacific Educational Research Conference. National Institute of Education. Singapore: 2008.

Valenta, C., and Kirchler, E. *Führung*. Vienna: 2011.

Varela, F., Thompson, E.; Rosch, E. *Der mittlere Weg der Erkenntnis. Der Brückenschlag zwischen wissenschaftlicher Theorie und menschlicher Erfahrung*. Bern: 1992.

Varga von Kibéd, M. Vorwort. In: de Shazer, S., and Dolan, Y. *Mehr als ein Wunder. Lösungsfokussierte Kurztherapie heute*. Heidelberg: Auer, 2008.

Vasek, T. *Die Weichmacher. Das süße Gift der Harmoniekultur*. Munich: 2011.

von Glasersfeld, E. Theorie der kognitiven Entwicklung. Ernst von Glasersfeld über das Werk von Jean Piaget – Einführung in die Genetische Epistemologie. *Pörksen*, (2011), 92–107.

von Hentig, H. *Die Schule neu denken. Eine Übung in praktischer Vernunft*. Munich: Hanser, 1993.

von Saldern, M. *Systemische Schulentwicklung*. Norderstedt: 2010.

von Schlippe, A. *Reflektierendes Team*. In: Wirth, J.; Kleve, H. (ed.). Lexikon des systemischen Arbeitens—Methodik und Theorie, Heidelberg. 2012, 328–331.

von Schlippe, A., and Schweitzer, J. *Lehrbuch der systemischen Therapie und Beratung*. Göttingen: 2003.

von Schlippe, A., and Schweitzer, J. *Systemische Interventionen*. Göttingen: 2009.

Watzlawick, P., Beavin, J.H., and Jackson, D.D. *Menschliche Kommunikation. Formen, Störungen, Paradoxien*. 4th ed. Bern: 1974.

Weber, G. (ed.). *Praxis der Organisationsaufstellungen. Grundlagen, Prinzipien, Anwendungsbereiche.* Heidelberg: 2002.

Weick, K.E., and Sutcliffe, K.M. *Das Unerwartete Managen. Wie Unternehmen aus Extremsituationen lernen.* 2nd ed. Stuttgart: 2010.

Willke, H. Strategien der Intervention in autonome Systeme. In: Baecker, D., Markowitz, J.; Stichweh, R.; Tyrell, H.; Willke, H. (ed.). *Theorie als Passion.* Frankfurt: 1987, 333–36.

Wirth, J.V., and Kleve, H. (ed.). *Lexikon des systemischen Arbeitens. Grundbegriffe der systemischen Praxis, Methodik und Theorie.* Heidelberg: 2012.

Wittgenstein, L. *Tractatus logico-philosophicus. Logisch-philosophische Abhandlung.* Frankfurt: 1963.

Zimmer, K. *Gefühle – unser erster Verstand.* Munich: 1999.

CPSIA information can be obtained at www.ICGtesting.com
Printed in the USA
BVOW01*0141130514

353310BV00002B/4/P